HEALTH SYSTEMS THINKING

A PRIMER

JAMES A. JOHNSON, PhD, MPA, MSc
Professor, School of Health Sciences
Central Michigan University
and
Visiting Professor, St. George's University
Grenada, West Indies

DOUGLAS E. ANDERSON, DHA, MSS, MBA, LFACHE
Adjunct Professor and Healthcare Consultant
Washington, DC Metro Area

CAREN C. ROSSOW, DHA, MSA, RN, FACHE
Assistant Professor, College of Health Sciences, Indiana University

JONES & BARTLETT
LEARNING

World Headquarters
Jones & Bartlett Learning
25 Mall Road
Burlington, MA 01803
978-443-5000
info@jblearning.com
www.jblearning.com

Jones & Bartlett Learning books and products are available through most bookstores and online booksellers. To contact Jones & Bartlett Learning directly, call 800-832-0034, fax 978-443-8000, or visit our website, www.jblearning.com.

Substantial discounts on bulk quantities of Jones & Bartlett Learning publications are available to corporations, professional associations, and other qualified organizations. For details and specific discount information, contact the special sales department at Jones & Bartlett Learning via the above contact information or send an email to specialsales@jblearning.com.

Production Credits
VP, Product Management: Amanda Martin
Director of Product Management: Michael Brown
Product Manager: Danielle Bessette
Production Manager: Carolyn Rogers Pershouse
Vendor Manager: Molly Hogue
Senior Marketing Manager: Susanne Walker
Manufacturing and Inventory Control Supervisor:
   Amy Bacus
Composition: codeMantra U.S. LLC

Project Management: codeMantra U.S. LLC
Cover Design: Kristin E. Parker
Director of Rights & Media: Joanna Gallant
Rights & Media Specialist: Merideth Tumasz
Media Development Editor: Shannon Sheehan
Cover Image (Title Page): © VIDOK/Getty Images
Printing and Binding: Gasch Printing
Cover Printing: Gasch Printing

Library of Congress Cataloging-in-Publication Data
Names: Johnson, James A., 1954- author. | Anderson, Douglas E., author. | Rossow, Caren C., author.
Title: Health systems thinking: a primer / James A. Johnson, Douglas E. Anderson, Caren C. Rossow.
Description: Burlington, MA: Jones & Bartlett Learning, [2020] | Includes bibliographical references and index.
Identifiers: LCCN 2018024966 | ISBN 9781284167146 (pbk.: alk. paper)
Subjects: | MESH: Delivery of Health Care—organization & administration | Systems Analysis | Systems Theory
Classification: LCC RA971 | NLM W 84.1 | DDC 362.1068—dc23
LC record available at https://lccn.loc.gov/2018024966

6048

Printed in the United States of America
24 23   10 9 8 7 6 5 4 3

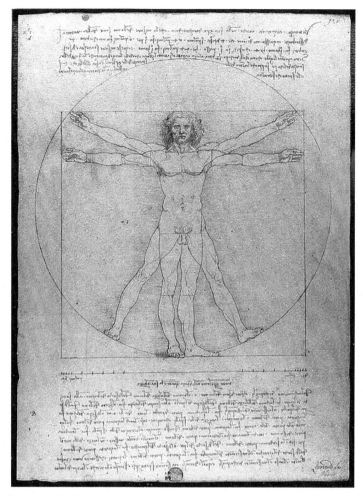

"I think with all my senses. When I have a vision of something, I can see it, I can touch it, I can taste it, I can smell it. I look for the hidden meaning behind everything, because I know that everything is connected with everything else."

Leonardo da Vinci (1452–1519), artist, inventor, scientist, systems thinker

Contents

Preface

In an era of a dynamic, uncertain, complex, and ambiguous health challenges at all levels and in every setting, this *Primer* on systems thinking, as it pertains to health, is urgently needed. Popularized 20 years ago, systems thinking principles and theories have waxed and waned in management and medical sciences, while retaining saliency in the physical, biological, and social sciences. Now, systems thinking has gained wide acceptance and applicability, especially in public health settings. It has been advocated by the World Health Organization, implemented at the Centers for Disease Control and Prevention, promoted by the American Medical Association, and utilized widely at the National Institutes of Health. Systems thinking challenges health leaders and clinicians to assess the interactions and interdependencies among elements in a system and seeks out opportunities to generate sustainable solutions. Furthermore, systems thinking focuses on nonlinear assumptions about human behavior and feedback loops to determine a system's behavior over time, thus finding leverage points to create more reliable and innovative health systems with a goal of better health for all. The theories, concepts, and methods presented in this text are suited to different health settings and professions. Furthermore, the *Primer* describes the foundations of systems thinking, while presenting tools, applications, and cases to enhance the readers' understanding and value of such an approach.

The *Primer* provides a foundations chapter to introduce the reader to systems theory, systems science, and systems thinking. This is followed by a chapter focused on systems thinking for health administration, a chapter on systems thinking for clinicians, and a subsequent chapter on systems thinking for public and global health. Each of these chapters includes essential concepts along with interviews of systems thinkers and illustrations of various systems thinking tools and processes. Finally, there is a fifth chapter that is comprised of systems thinking cases selected to profile a sample of systems thinking applications in a variety of settings addressing diverse challenges and problems.

Currently, the accrediting commissions within public health, health administration, and nursing are including systems thinking as part of the core competencies in their respective fields. Likewise, in medicine, we are seeing health systems science being added to the medical curricula. Meanwhile, academic programs do not have sufficient learning materials on this topic to give students the requisite knowledge expected of the next generation of health professionals. This *Primer* addresses the void by empowering its readers with greater understanding of this important and timely topic, while increasing appreciation for the tremendous potential and urgent necessity of systems thinking.

In an April 16, 2018 *Time Magazine* interview with Bill Gates, founder of Microsoft and Co-President of the Bill and Melinda Gates Foundation, Mr. Gates made the following statement about systems:

> Modernity is a miracle of systems. Jonas Salk was an amazing scientist, but he isn't the only reason we're on the doorstep of eradicating polio—it's also thanks to the coordinated vaccination effort of health workers, NGOs, and governments. We miss the progress that's happening right in front of us when we look for heroes instead of systems. If you want to improve something, look for ways to build better systems.

With the publication of this health systems thinking primer, we hope to inspire and empower you to do just that in your organization, profession, and the world.

James A. Johnson, PhD, MPA, MSc

About the Authors

Dr. James A. Johnson is a medical social scientist and health policy analyst who specializes in organizational and systems development. He is a Full Professor in the School of Health Sciences at Central Michigan University where he teaches comparative health systems and health systems thinking. Dr. Johnson is also a Visiting Professor at St. George's University in Grenada, West Indies and the former Chairman of the Department of Health Administration and Policy at the Medical University of South Carolina where he was also an Associate Professor of Family Medicine. He has been an active researcher and health science writer with 18 books and over 100 journal articles published. Fifteen of his books are in the National Library of Medicine. One recent book, which is read worldwide, is titled *Comparative Health Systems: Global Perspectives* where he and co-researchers analyzed the health systems of 20 different countries. Dr. Johnson is the past-editor of the American College of Healthcare Executives (ACHE) *Journal of Healthcare Management*; founding editor of the *Carolina Health Services Review*; currently a Contributing Editor for the *Journal of Health and Human Services Administration*, and global health editor for the *Journal of Human Security and Resilience*. He works closely with the World Health Organization (WHO) in Geneva, Switzerland and the Heart to Heart NGO in Belize, on projects, often involving students. He is a regular voting delegate to the World Health Congress. His work and travels have taken him to 40 countries so far. Dr. Johnson has been an invited lecturer at Oxford University (England); Beijing University (China); University of Dublin (Ireland); University of Colima (Mexico); St. George's University (Grenada) and University of Pretoria (South Africa), as well as, universities, associations, and health organizations within the United States, including visiting or adjunct professorships at University of Michigan and Auburn University. Additionally, he serves on the Governing Council of the American Public Health Association (APHA) and has served on many boards including the Scientific Advisory Board of the National Diabetes Trust Foundation; Board of the Association of University Programs in Health Administration (AUPHA); Advisory Board of the Alliance for the Blind and Visually Impaired; Board President of Charleston Lowcountry AIDS Services; Advisory Board of the Joint Africa Working Group; Board of Directors of the Africa Research and Development Center; Advisory Board of the Center for Collaborative Health Leadership; and Board of Advisors for Health Systems of America. He is assisting the Kenya Relief NGO with the formation of an international advisory board. Dr. Johnson completed his PhD at Florida State University where he specialized in health policy and organization development. He also has an MPA in healthcare administration and policy from Auburn University.

Douglas E. Anderson is a retired Air Force Medical Service Corps officer and currently serves as consultant and adjunct professor. He coaches senior health executives on strategic leadership and provides customized leader development programs.

He has experience as a CEO, COO, and Corp. Staff officer and worked many large-scale transformational initiatives throughout his career. Prior to retirement, he served as the Director of Strategic Communication for the AF Surgeon General and spent 1-year helping the Afghanistan National Police build their health system. He is co-author of *Systems Thinking for Health Organizations, Leadership, and Policy.*

Dr. Caren C. Rossow is an Assistant Professor of healthcare administration at the Vera Z. Dwyer College of Health Sciences, Judd Leighton School of Business, and the College of Liberal Arts and Sciences at Indiana University of South Bend. Currently, Dr. Rossow teaches graduate and undergraduate courses in healthcare management, health policy and advocacy, ethics, and healthcare human resource management. Prior to her academic appointment, she worked over 30 years in a number of divisions and director and management positions in community hospitals and regional healthcare systems. She has a comprehensive background in various healthcare service lines and is experienced in planning, operations, logistics, finance, and human resource management. After completing her doctorate, she has presented internationally and authored peer-reviewed articles and book chapters. She is co-author with James Johnson on the recently published second edition of *Health Organization: Theory Behavior, and Development.* Her research interests include international health, pandemics, health systems in crisis, and organizational and biomedical ethics. Dr. Rossow has participated in 12 study abroad and service learning trips to five countries, most recently co-leading trips to both Sweden and Belize. Dr. Rossow completed an MSA at the College of Business, University of Notre Dame, and a CIH (Certificate in International Health) and DHA at the Dow College of Health Professions, Central Michigan University. Dr. Rossow is also a registered nurse (RN) and a Fellow in the American College of Healthcare Executives (FACHE).

CHAPTER 1

Introduction to Systems Thinking

▶ Systems Theory and Foundations

Systems theory has its roots in ancient times and philosophy dating back thousands of years. There is evidence of the embrace of systems theory in Chinese, Persian, Egyptian, and Greek writings. More recently, the world was introduced to the paradigm shifting work of a German-Canadian biologist and philosopher Ludwig von Bertalanffy with the publication in 1968 of his book titled *General Systems Theory*.[1] Inspired by this theory, in the 1970s, physician George Engel developed the "biopsychosocial model" as an expression of systems thinking for understanding disease. Systems thinking inspired many professionals in medical, nursing, and health education to advance the model's fundamental assumption that illness is based on the interplay of biological, psychological, and social factors (**FIGURE 1.1**).

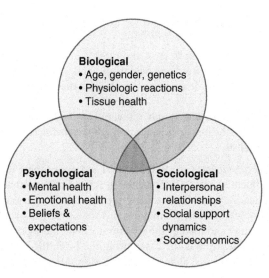

FIGURE 1.1 Biopsychosocial Model

It has now become more acceptable within and across the full spectrum of health science and practice. However, the expression of General Systems Theory continues to be emergent in myriad and novel ways, as you will see in the chapters of this text.

General Systems Theory

General Systems Theory or the unified "science of wholeness" was initiated by von Bertalanffy for two reasons: (1) a reaction against reductionism and (2) an effort to unite the fields of science. Reductionism, which is grounded in the work of Descartes and Newton, is when anything in the natural world or society is studied by examining its individual parts. This was the dominant viewpoint in the 19th and 20th centuries. Reductionism has an influential place in scientific research but it only goes so far, often simply seeking to understand how the parts work in an attempt to extrapolate an understanding of the whole. However, many investigators in the early days of scientific study failed to look at the system as a whole or see how all the parts were interconnected and interdependent. Unfortunately, this is still too often the case today.

Opposing the notion of reductionism that has dominated much of the history of science, von Bertalanffy theorized that systems are open to and interact with their environments. For example, instead of reducing the human body to the properties of its parts, systems theory focuses on the relationship between the parts that make them a whole functioning entity, including interconnected subsystems, organs, microbiome, genes, and biochemicals. Bertalanffy's desire was to unite the different fields of science such as physics, biology, chemistry, physiology, psychology, and others under a framework by which each could contribute to the understanding of natural phenomena and, by extension, human-created phenomena such as societies and organizations. To advance this quest, in 1954, he and colleagues from the American Association for the Advancement of Science organized the Society for General Systems Research "to further the development of theoretical systems which are applicable to more than one of the traditional departments of knowledge."[1] The primary functions of the society were to:

1. Investigate concepts, laws, and models in various fields and help in the useful transfer from one field to another.
2. Encourage the development of adequate theoretical models in fields that lack them.
3. Minimize the duplication of theoretical effort in different fields.
4. Promote the unity of science through improving communication among specialists.

Less than a decade later, in 1962, physicist and philosopher of science Thomas Kuhn in his influential book *The Structure of Scientific Revolutions* introduced the concept of a scientific "paradigm" to describe an underlying framework for a constellation of concepts, values, techniques, methods, and perspectives shared by a scientific community and used by the community to define legitimate problems and solutions.[2] This certainly was the case during the Scientific Revolution when the dominant paradigm was well aligned with reductionist thinking, mechanistic thinking, and the long shadow of Sir Isaac Newton's influential work *Principia* published in 1687. However, the centuries-old paradigm has now given way to newer thought in quantum physics, neurophysiology, complexity science, cosmology, and artificial intelligence. Most pertinent to this Primer and the topic of systems thinking is the embrace of the new paradigm of systems theory by the social and medical sciences. As world-renowned physicist Fritjof Capra asserts in his book *The Systems View of Life: A Unifying Vision*, "Physics, together with chemistry is essential to understand the behavior of the molecules in living cells, but it is not sufficient to describe their self-organizing patterns and processes. The new scientific understanding of life at all levels of living systems—organisms, social systems, and ecosystems—is based on a perception of reality that has profound implications not only for science and philosophy, but also for politics, business, healthcare, education, and many other areas of everyday life."[3]

Systems theory has become more widespread in North America within academia, especially in the biological sciences and social sciences. In the spirit of systems theory as a unifying theory for all of the sciences, systemologist and computer scientist Gene Bellinger, founder of the Systems Thinking World Initiative, underscores von Bertalanffy's paradigm of General Systems Theory as follows: "There are fundamental structures which act across all branches of science. And, if one learns the structures, when transferring from one discipline to another, much of the learning can be transferred. When studying a new discipline, one would simply have to learn the labels on the structures in the new discipline. General Systems Theory, therefore, proposes the universe is full of systems, and each system differs from the next. There are universal laws or principles that can be applied to all of them. If you learn about these universal laws, you can apply them to a specific system. A science of wholeness, General Systems Theory looks at the universe holistically rather than in parts. It is, in simplest terms, a way to understand how things work by looking for patterns responsible for behaviors and events."[4] In a more condensed statement, Bellinger asserts, "A system is an entity that maintains its existence through the mutual interaction of its parts"[4] or as Anderson and Johnson state, "A system is a group of interacting, interrelated, or interdependent components that form a complex and unified whole."[5] A systems components might be physical, but they can also be less tangible such as processes, relationships, policies, and information.

Medical social scientist James Johnson provides in *Comparative Health Systems* a useful analogy that anyone in the health professions can easily relate to: "The human body is a system composed of many physiological subsystems that are interconnected in a holistic way. The subsystems, including respiratory, circulatory, neurological, endocrine, and musculoskeletal system, communicate and are interdependent. They work together for the purposes of survival, adaptation, growth, and development. They interact with the environment and respond to feedback from within and outside the system. In many ways, the interconnectivity of the various subsystems and its extension as a whole into the environment form the building blocks of larger systems, such as family, community, and nation."[6] In other words, people live and work within systems, while at the same time, they themselves are systems, as are the organizations in which they work.

Systems Theory of Organization

In *Health Organizations*, Johnson and Rossow assert that organizational researchers have often adopted a reductionist approach to understanding organizations that have not changed much since the 1911 publication of Frederick Taylor's *The Principles of Scientific Management*.[7,8] In this classical paradigm, organizational problems are addressed by finding the "weak link" and fixing the "part" that is "broken." However, through the lens of systems theory, organizations can be viewed as *complex adaptive systems* (CASs), and not "machines" of assembled parts. After all, health care and public health are complex in that they are composed of multiple, diverse, interconnected elements, and equally important, they are dynamic in that they are capable of changing and learning from experience and their environments. As shown by Johnson, Stoskopf, and Shi, in a comparative study involving more than 25 countries, this complexity seems to be the case worldwide in a variety of health systems and organizational contexts.[6]

Most organizations and certainly all health organizations can be described as CASs that are constantly adjusting to their environments and responding to feedback from within and without the environments. Complexity science sees change as inevitable and, thus, the search for a stable state is futile. Being open to exchanges and interactions with the environment, CASs continuously adjust to moment-by-moment perturbations and other inputs from within and without and from outside the system.[7]

CASs have attributes that are consistent with General Systems Theory and the newly emerging complexity science. These attributes are described in **BOX 1.1**.

BOX 1.1   Attributes of Complex Adaptive Systems

McDaniel RR and Jordan ME. Complexity and Postmodern Theory. In: Johnson JA. *Health Organizations*. Jones and Bartlett Publishers; 2009.

Agents (i.e., People)

CASs consist of a large number of diverse agents that are information processors. There must be adequate diversity within the group of agents to enable the group to develop new solutions to problems and make decisions in unique circumstances. In CAS, agents have the capacity to exchange information among themselves and with their environment and adjust their own behavior as a function of the information they process. In a health organization, everyone counts; not only does each person contribute his or her talents but the individual must also help others contribute. Managing such a diverse and changing cast of agents are considered most difficult among other tasks in healthcare management.

Interconnections

The essence of CAS is captured in the nonlinear relationships among agents. Inputs are not proportional to outputs; small changes can lead to big effects and big changes can lead to small effects. The way in which clinicians interact with each other, coupled with the way they interact with nonclinicians, is often a key determinant of a health organization's ability to succeed. Everyone is busy and everyone has his or her job to do. CAS theory teaches us that the successful healthcare manager pays more attention to the relationship system than to the individual agents.

Self-Organization

CAS theory teaches us that order in a system may well be a result of the properties of the system itself, rather than some intentionality on the part of some external controller.

Rather than hierarchical control, CASs are characterized by a decentralized, bottom-up process of co-design. New structures and new forms of behavior spontaneously emerge as agents self-organize themselves into relatively stable patterns of relationships. No matter how hard a nursing home manager tries to control certified nursing attendants, the attendants will organize themselves to do their job in the way that they see fit. Efforts to help them better perceive and perform their job and develop effective organizational analytical skills are likely to pay greater dividends than efforts to get them to simply comply.

Emergence

The behavior of CAS cannot be obtained by summing the behaviors of the constituent parts but emerges as the result of the pattern of connections among diverse agents. Emergence is a source of novelty and surprise in CAS. When we treat safety and clinical success as emergent properties of the system, we are more likely to learn from the past behaviors of the system and develop alternative strategies for achieving our goals.

Co-evolution

CASs do not simply change; they change the world around. CAS and its environments co-evolve such that each fundamentally influences the development of the other. The organizations act and others react, often in unexpected and unpredictable ways. When a health organization begins to investigate the purchase of some new information technology, the potential ramifications will almost immediately come to the fore in the decision-making process. When a big payer decides that you should be paid by a system using diagnostic-related groups, you will figure out how to code the illnesses of your clients so that it is profitable for you.

As described by Johnson and Anderson, there are additional defining characteristics of complex systems that should be considered[9]:

1. *Complex systems tend to be self-stabilizing.* A systems likely contains many balancing feedback loops, each of which serves to keep some smaller component or subsystem in balance with the larger more complex system. An example would be the various units of the National Institutes of Health remaining on the cutting edge of research within their domain while also serving the larger purpose and mission of medical research.[9]

2. *Complex systems are purposeful.* These systems often seem to function with a mind of their own. An example of this is the work of the Red Cross in a disaster relief effort.

3. *Complex systems are capable of using feedback to modify their behavior.* All systems do this, providing an essential opportunity for adaptation and innovation. An example would be a health department forming a partnership with an AIDS organization to better provide access to HIV testing.

4. *Complex systems can modify their environments.* Systems can modify their behavior to achieve goals or fulfill a purpose. In doing so, due to the interconnection of everything, they also alter their environments. Concomitant with the change in a systems behavior is the need to identify the links between the system and its environment. An example

would be using systems thinking to address water quality issues in a community such as Flint, Michigan.[9]

5. *Complex systems are capable of replicating, maintaining, repairing, and organizing themselves.* This is sometimes referred to as reengineering, reinvention, or organizational transformation. An example of health care would be the incredible growth in scope and scale of the Cleveland Clinics over the last decade.[9]

▶ Systems Thinking

Many would trace the popularization of the concept of systems thinking to the 1990 publication of Peter Senge's *The Fifth Discipline*.[10] The book quickly became a worldwide bestseller, in part, because it resonated with our own innate understanding of organizations as systems and, even more so, of organization as an entity capable of learning. In fact, the subtitle for the book was "The Art and Practice of the Learning Organization." As a management professor at MIT, Senge became a strident advocate for the use of systems thinking to facilitate learning at the organizational and individual levels. Almost prophetically, 30 years ago, he stated, "Today, systems thinking is needed more than ever because we are becoming overwhelmed by complexity. Perhaps for the first time in history, humankind has the capacity to create far more information than anyone can absorb, to foster far greater interdependency than anyone can manage, and to accelerate change far faster than anyone's ability to keep pace."[10]

To many, especially professors and social scientists, as well as practicing managers and leaders at all levels of organizations, Senge effectively introduced a new language. He called it "a shift of mind" and introduced mental models that could help foster our understanding of the systems paradigm.

Mental Models and Systems Language

One of the overarching mental models is systems thinking, which according to Senge, "offers a language that begins by restructuring how we think."[10] Language is one of the most distinguishing characteristics of what it means to be human. It certainly shapes how we relate to others and has for millennia. In *Elements of Social Scientific Thinking*, Hoover and Donovan describe the importance of language as follows:

> After several thousand years of human history, we still have to face the fact that the process of naming things is difficult. Language emerges essentially by agreement. You and I and the other members of the family (tribe, state, nation, world) agree for example to call things that twinkle in the sky *stars*. Unfortunately, these agreements may not be precise. In common usage, the term "star" covers a multitude of objects, big and small, hot and cold, solid and gaseous. To call a thing by a precise name is the beginning of understanding, because it is the key to the procedure that allows the mind to grasp reality and its many relationships. It makes a great deal of difference whether an illness is conceived of as caused by an evil spirit or by a bacteria on a binge. The concept *bacteria* is tied to a system of concepts in which there is a connection to a powerful repertoire of treatments, that is, antibiotics.[11]

So, what then is the language of this emergent paradigm we call systems thinking? James Johnson and Douglas Anderson provide an answer from their perspective:

> Systems thinking is a set of tools and a way of thinking involving new language. In systems thinking, one looks at the whole system rather than its individual parts. This prompts thought to become expansive and nonlinear in perspective rather than reductionist and linear. By looking at the whole, one becomes more capable of seeing interrelationships and patterns over time. This helps begin the understanding that problems may be clues or symptomatic of deeper issues. Systems thinking challenges organizational leaders and health professionals to look for root causes, bottlenecks, and constraints in ways that might preclude sustainable solutions to emerge. By doing so, leaders move away from assigning blame and instead focus on desired outcomes.[9]

Furthermore, Johnson and Anderson perceive systems thinking as proactive, open, and circular in nature, differing from linear thinking, which tends to be reactive.[9] This is explored further in their book *Systems Thinking for Health Organizations, Leadership and Policy*, in which the authors provide a summation of fundamental systems thinking perspectives, assumptions, and possible solutions to a complex public health challenge—substance abuse and addiction.

First, systems thinking reframes conversations to help others see "whole" systems, not "silos" in isolation. Systems thinking challenges everyone to identify patterns, interrelationships, and boundaries beyond the issue of the moment. Complex, ongoing, and chronic problems such as preventable deaths from drug overdose require a systems approach to reducing harm, perhaps by changing prescription practices as well as effective education and law enforcement practices, along with myriad other possible solutions.

Second, viewing the problem as a whole system in a larger context does not favor breaking down problems into small segments. Systems thinking prompts investigation and systemic assessment, through the "viewpoints" of all stakeholders, no exceptions. Systems thinking urges leaders to connect with and mobilize others as a team to recognize and utilize interconnections needed for impactful and sustainable solutions. For example, ending the opioid epidemic has interconnected medical, behavioral, public health, and social viewpoints, and solutions. This would go beyond Engel's biopsychosocial model to a more comprehensive approach that includes health system science currently being promoted by the American Medical Association (AMA) and various professional associations. Systems thinking helps stakeholders see dysfunctional patterns and interactions of their "silos" and the impact on the system as a whole.

Third, systems thinking is a transformational way of understanding and approaching community-based solutions. By seeing the trends, interactions, and connections at the individual, team, organizational, community, or national levels, leaders understand more fully the need for systemic approaches to solve problems rather than generate solutions in isolation. For example, health executives and physicians need to understand how social determinants of health, including community culture and demographics, will affect the desired outcomes. Conversely, public health practitioners and policymakers should understand how the population health component of the Triple Aim, or the "Quadruple Aim," could support an initiative aimed at reducing substance abuse or better managing addiction.

Finally, systems analysis examines complex challenges using systems thinking tools and methodologies. The systems approach requires us to view problems within an organization, community, or country and examine all of the interactions, interdependences, and interrelations connected with those issues. For example, the challenge of addiction, at both personal and societal levels, necessitates the embrace of systems thinking as the best, and perhaps only, way to look at all of the elements of the whole, coupled with the dynamics (interconnections) that are at play.

From these examples, one can begin to get a feel for the language of systems thinking and understand why it adds value to intervention in complex health challenges. Another example is the use of systems thinking to better understand and mitigate the problems of tobacco use and health. Richard Reigelman provides an example of this in his description of the collaboration between the National Cancer Institute and the Institute of Medicine (**BOX 1.2**).

BOX 1.2 Smoking from a Systems Thinking Versus Reductionist Thinking Perspective

The work of the National Cancer Institute and the Institute of Medicine on tobacco control encourages a systems thinking approach. Systems thinking is more easily understood by contrasting it with the traditional approach, which has been called the reductionist approach. The following three concepts are key to understanding the differences between systems thinking and reductionist thinking:

1. One intervention at a time versus multiple simultaneous interventions
   A reductionist approach attempts to look at one factor or intervention at a time. An intervention, such as a smoking cessation program, might be investigated to determine whether it works when used alone. Rather than looking at one intervention at a time, systems thinking asks about the best combination of interventions. Systems thinking might identify smoking cessation programs, social marketing, and higher taxes as three important compatible interventions that need to be effectively and efficiently combined.
2. Straight-line or linear projections versus measuring complex interactions
   A reductionist approach usually assumes a straight-line or linear relationship implying that increased levels of an intervention, such as increasing taxes on tobacco, will produce a straight-line decrease in the levels of tobacco use. However, it is possible that small increases in taxes have little effect, while slightly larger increases have dramatic effects. In addition, reductionist approaches do not look at how the impact of one intervention may be affected by connecting it with other interventions, whereas systems thinking looks at these interactions. Thus, systems thinking would ask questions about how to most effectively utilize cigarette taxes by combining them with other approaches, such as using the taxes to support tobacco education programs or reducing exposure to radon, asbestos, or other causes of lung cancer.
3. One-point-in-time or static analysis versus a changing or dynamic analysis
   Reductionist approaches look at the relationships at one point in time. That is, they use static models and do not consider changes that often occur over time. For instance, they would not look at how changes in social attitudes over time may alter the effectiveness of tobacco cessation programs or set the stage for enforcement of public smoking regulations or increased tobacco taxes. Rather than seeing interventions as static or at one point in time, systems thinking

> develops dynamic models that look at the feedback process, the changes that occur over time, and bottlenecks that slow down change. For instance, systems thinking might identify a need to train large numbers of clinicians in smoking cessation methods so that they can address the demand for smoking cessation services created by social marketing, increased cigarette taxes, and better drug treatments.

As you can see from this description, the language of systems thinking mental model does, in fact, contribute to the shift in mindset that is reflective of the fundamentals of General Systems Theory.

Health Systems Thinking

In the rapidly changing domains of public health and healthcare delivery systems worldwide, systems thinking can be perceived as offering valuable insights for understanding and action. The World Health Organization (WHO) describes systems thinking as "an approach to problem solving that views 'problems' as part of a wider, dynamic system. Systems thinking involves much more than a reaction to present outcomes or events. It demands a deeper understanding of the linkages, relationships, interactions, and behaviors among the elements to characterize the entire system."[12]

The WHO definition of a health system includes the sum total of all the organizations, institutions, and resources whose primary purpose is to improve health. As a precursor to the systems view of health, in 1948, the agency described health as follows: "a state of complete physical, mental, and social well-being and not merely the absence of disease or infirmary."[6] This is still the most widely used definition of health and is embraced by most of the Ministries of Health in countries throughout the world. To help assure this, the WHO has fully embraced systems thinking and promotes it worldwide. Their best-known publication on the topic is *Systems Thinking for Health Systems Strengthening* with the collaboration of the Alliance for Health Policy and Systems Research.[12]

The AMA, another highly influential organization, recently released a publication titled *Health Systems Science*, which not only describes systems thinking in the medical practice context but also advocates including systems science in medical school curricula alongside basic and clinical sciences. As stated, "Even if the basic and clinical sciences are expertly learned and executed, without health systems science, physicians cannot realize their full potential on patients' health or on the population."[13]

In their book *Applied Systems Thinking for Health Systems Research*, de Savigny and colleagues argue that conventional reductionist approaches to epidemiologic and implementation research are inadequate for tackling many of the emerging challenges faced by health systems around the world. They, in turn, call for a systems thinking approach that is more likely to lead to actionable results by appropriately identifying critical problems and questions.

▶ Concepts and Methods of Systems Thinking

Given the range of sciences that have embraced systems thinking, there has been a dramatic proliferation of concepts and tools that are being used. Much of this

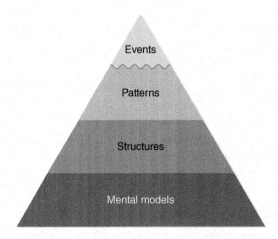

FIGURE 1.2 Systems Thinking Pyramid

has been led by physics, especially quantum physics, and the biological sciences. However, the social sciences and health sciences have also been major contributors to this expansion in the scope of systems thinking. In addition to its growing use in medical education, systems theory is widely used in schools of social work, schools of nursing, schools of management, and increasingly schools of public health.

Perhaps the most fundamental image that captures the essence of systems thinking is the pyramid shown in **FIGURE 1.2**, which identifies levels of awareness and analysis that are essential to the understanding of human phenomena, such as health and illness.

Systems Thinking Concepts

There are core concepts within the systems paradigm that seem to be universal and thus transdisciplinary. Brief descriptions of some of these are as follows:

> *Unintended consequences* are the all too common experiences of an action not yielding the desired result. Instead, there might be the unintended outcome of a decision or intervention. From a systems perspective, this commonly occurs because the actor has not fully understood the underlying systems dynamics or patterns. An example of this would be a decision to purchase a new piece of equipment, and then it is underused or not used at all.

> *Emergence* from a systems perspective is when larger things emerge from smaller parts: Emergence is the natural outcome of things coming together as a result of the synergies of the parts. An example of this is how a functioning human body emerges from the synergy of a multitude of small cells.

> *Feedback* is the return of information about the status of a process or situation. An example would be the annual performance review providing information to a physical therapist about the quality of his or her work, which could also include feedback from patients or physical therapy assistants.

Equifinality is the principle that a system can reach a given end state or goal by various means or routes. An example would be the ability to raise $100,000 for a health foundation through donors or through grants.

Resilience is the ability of a system to recover from disturbances and disruptions, including the ability to repair or restore itself after a change due to an outside force. Systemologist Dana Meadows says, "Resilience is a measure of a system's ability to survive and persist within a variable environment."[14] Meadows provides an example of noncommunicable disease, such as cancer, resulting from a breakdown of resilience mechanisms that repair DNA or control cell division.[14]

Self-organization is the ability of a system to structure itself, create new structure, learn, or diversify. The learning organization, as described by Senge earlier in this chapter, is a good example.[10]

Nonlinearity is when the relationship between two elements in a system is not linear (a constant proportion between cause and effect also known graphically as a straight-line effect). Nonlinearity can never result in a straight line from cause to effect. An example would be a weather pattern such as a hurricane.

Bounded rationality means that people make reasonable decisions based on the information they have, but they do not have complete or perfect information. The decision might make sense in one part of a system but is not reasonable when seen from a whole system perspective. For example, a health insurance exchange might work in one state but might not be effective on a national level.

Interconnection refers to the degree of interrelatedness, coordination, and collaboration among components or levels of a system. This is a measure of complexity and functional coupling of subcomponents. An example would be the many levels of individuals, health professionals, family members, and community health and social services all connected to produce better health for the population.

Flow is the amount of change something undergoes during a particular length of time; for example, the amount of water that flows out of a faucet each minute is also known as the rate of change. This is commonly seen in the form of medical materials being used or in the amount of information being shared.

Leverage points are those places where small changes can result in larger results. A leverage point is a place in the system's structure where an intervention can be applied. A low leverage point is one where a small level of intervention or change force results in a small change in the behavior of the system. In contrast, a high leverage point is one where a small level of intervention/change force causes a large change in the system's behavior. In the economics of health behavior, leverage points can be in the form of incentives, such as reduced insurance premiums if you quit smoking.

System trap is a way of thinking that is inappropriate for the context or issue being explored.

This is a fairly concise grouping of systems concepts, as the theory and application of systems thinking continue to emerge from work being done in systems science, social sciences, neurobiology, theoretical physics, artificial intelligence, and perhaps every field of applied science, as they shift their mental models for the future. Likewise, beyond the sciences in the realms of policy and diplomacy, there is an increasing embrace of systems concepts to better understand the world.

Systems Thinking Tools and Methods

There are many systems thinking tools commonly used to measure, map, and visualize these concepts. Some of the commonly used tools are diagramed in **FIGURE 1.3**.

BOX 1.3 provides a summary of a few of systems thinking tools that you are likely to see in the systems science literature, as well as in subsequent chapters of this text.

In addition to the graphic and visual systems tools described earlier, systems thinking uses certain mental models as conceptual tools to help understand systems behavior and dynamics. Borrowing from the term used by Swiss psychologist Carl Jung to describe universals or collective symbols, Peter Senge applied the concept to systems thinking as a way to describe common patterns that occur repeatedly in organizations in different settings and at different times.[10] More recently, Johnson and Anderson define systems archetypes as mental models representing recurring patterns of behavior or outcomes, both negative and positive.[9] The authors caution, unless uncovered earlier rather than later, these patterns may result in unintended

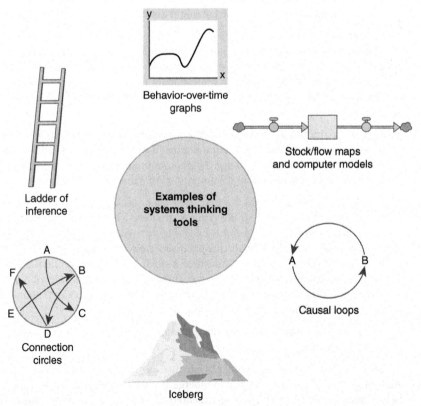

Behavior-over-time
graphs

Stock/flow maps
and computer models

Ladder of
inference

**Examples of
systems thinking
tools**

Connection
circles

Causal loops

Iceberg

FIGURE 1.3 Systems Thinking Tools

BOX 1.3 Common Systems Thinking Tools

Behavior Over Time (BOT) Diagram: BOT diagrams capture the history or a future trend of one or more variables over time. By sketching the variables on the same graph over time, an explicit understanding of how they interact over time is acquired.

Causal Loop Diagram (CLD): CLDs capture how variables in a system are interrelated. An CLD takes the form of one or more closed loops to depict cause-and-effect linkages that capture how variables in a system are interrelated.

Stock and Flow Diagrams: Stock and flow diagrams are quantitative systems dynamics tools used for illustrating a system that can be used for model-based policy analysis in a simulated, dynamic environment. Stock and flow diagrams explicitly incorporate feedback to understand complex systems behavior and capture nonlinear dynamics.

Feedback Loops: These illustrate self-perpetuating mechanism of change and response to that change. The return of information about the status of a process is a form of interconnection. Reinforcing or amplifying feedback loops drives growth or creates a decline in system performance at any level. They either spiral up or down. They rarely occur in isolation within a system (team, organization, or community). However, a loop can move in either a positive or a negative direction, depending on capacity and quality of interactions in a system.

Balancing Feedback Loop: These help diminish the effect of disturbances or interventions.

Reinforcing Loop/Process: Along with balancing loops, this forms the two building blocks of dynamic systems. Reinforcing processes produce both growth and collapse—they compound change in one direction with even more change. A reinforcing loop depicts a reinforcing process.

Balancing Loop/Process: A balancing loop depicts a balancing process. Balancing processes seek equilibrium or try to bring things to a desired state and keep them there.

Graphical Function Diagram (GFD): GFDs show how one variable interacts with another (such as the effect of delivery delays on quality of care) by plotting the relationship between the two over the entire range of relevant values (e.g., drug outages or restrictive formularies delay decisions and application) and results in poorer recovery times and outcomes. The resulting diagram is a concise hypothesis of how the two variables interrelate.

consequences or frustration that can spread to other parts of a system and potentially throughout the entire system. Some of the systems archetypes likely to be found in organizations, including health organizations, are as follows:

Tragedy of the Commons (Archetype) occurs when a shared resource becomes overburdened as each person in the system uses more resource for themselves. Eventually, the resource is diminished or depleted. The classic example is a water well in a village where rain cannot replenish the underground aquifer fast enough to keep up with use of the well.

Shifting the Burden (Archetype) is when a short-term solution is tried that successfully solves an ongoing problem. As the solution is used repeatedly, it takes attention away from more fundamental solutions. Over time, the ability to apply a fundamental solution may decrease, resulting in a greater reliance on the symptomatic solution. A well-known example is drug or alcohol dependency in response to stress.

Balancing Loop/Process with Delay (Archetype) occurs when a balancing process has a long delay, the usual response is to overcorrect, leading to wild swings in behavior. An example observed in hospitals and clinics would be low inventory of medical supplies causing the staff to overstock or hoard to the point of waste.

Success to the Successful (Archetype) occurs in situations where two activities compete for a common but limited resource. The more successful activity is consistently given more resources, allowing it to succeed even more, while the less successful one becomes starved for resources and eventually dies out. An example might be a scenario where two urgent care clinics from two different health systems compete for the same population base.

Fixes that Fail (Archetype): In this situation, a fix or correction is applied to a problem that has immediate positive results but has unforeseen long-term consequences that eventually make the problem worse. An example too often seen with the obesity epidemic is severe dieting that then leads to nutritional deficiency.

Eroding Goals (Archetype): In this scenario, a gradual downward slide in performance goals goes unnoticed, threatening the long-term future of the system or organization. One possible example would be the focus of healthcare executives on profit margins at the expense of patient safety.

Escalation (Archetype): In this archetype, two parties compete for superiority in an arena. As one party's actions move ahead, the other party "retaliates" by increasing its actions. The result is a continual ratcheting up of activity on both sides. An example would be two physicians worried about their turf and ego arguing constantly while the CEO does not have the confidence to intervene.

▶ Systems Thinking Application

To give the reader of this Primer a sample of the use of systems thinking in understanding and addressing a current and challenging health systems issue, we have invited a guest author who engages in consulting with health organizations worldwide. The article was written and contributed by Stephen M. Powell, Founder and President of the Atlanta-based global consulting firm Synensys, LLC. Coincidently (or perhaps not), given the focus of this text, the name of Steve's firm is derived from the words "systems" and "synthesis" (**BOX 1.4**). Additionally, he is the author of *The Patient Survival Handbook: Avoid Being the Next Victim of Medical Error.*[15]

BOX 1.4 Systems Thinking for Patient Safety

Contributing Author: Stephen M. Powell

According to Johnson and Anderson, systems thinking "focuses on non-linear assumptions about human behavior and feedback loops to determine a systems behavior over time to find leverage points to create the most reliable and innovative health systems that are sustainable with a goal of better health for all."[9] Systems thinking is perfectly suited to address intransient, complex, and seemingly unsolvable problems such as patient safety.

Some estimates suggest that preventable adverse events have become the third leading cause of death in the United States, placing medical errors behind only heart disease and cancer.[16] In the Institute of Medicine (IOM) report *To Err Is Human*, initial estimates of deaths in the United States due to medical errors were reported to be between 44,000 and 98,000 lives each year. The current estimated loss of lives is 400,000 annually—a nearly 10-fold increase over the initial IOM estimates in 2000.[16] Of course, some of the differences may be attributed to mortality surveillance and reporting.[16]

Following the IOM report, healthcare organizations across the United States have launched patient safety programs and interventions to reduce preventable adverse events; however, the pace of improvement is painstakingly slow and often unsustainable over time.[17] The IOM report suggested that medicine and related professions take a "systems approach" to improving patient safety similar to other high-risk industries such as aviation and the nuclear power industry.[18] Health professionals have turned to safety principles attributed to High Reliability Organizations (HROs) that can achieve extremely low incidence in risky situations.[19] Many cross-disciplinary practitioners, researchers, and policymakers began adopting these practices and programs in higher risk healthcare settings, such as operating rooms, intensive care units, emergency departments, and obstetrical care settings. Most programs have focused primarily on training with weaker attempts to change behavior over time, which is necessary in systems thinking. This circumstance begs the question: Is it time to reframe the patient safety problem as a systems problem, requiring systems thinking and a systems approach?

Patient Safety as a System

Emanuel and colleagues submitted a working model or framework to begin viewing patient safety as a system rather than isolated or silo episodes of disjointed care delivery.[20] **FIGURE 1.4** illustrates the model showing its embrace of systems thinking design, human

FIGURE 1.4 Patient Safety Systems Model

(continues)

BOX 1.4 Systems Thinking for Patient Safety   *(continued)*

factors, and other systems engineering disciplines along with feedback loops to monitor continuously and improve systems performance. The model shows four interactive elements within patient safety: patients (the recipients of care), healthcare workers (the professionals who deliver care), healthcare systems (the therapeutic care enablers), and the methods of monitoring and improving care (continuous quality improvement). Unfortunately, human failures at the point of care have resulted in a culture of blame and shame among healthcare professionals ("bad" people versus poorly functioning systems).

The dotted lines in the model represent the complex interaction or "permeability" between patient safety systems and stakeholders.[20] Patients and their families are more integrally linked in the practice of safe care than passengers on an airliner or customers of a nuclear power plant due to social determinants of health such as access to prescribed medications and follow-up care after discharge. Patients and families, when possible, must take an active role in the patients' care team advocating for safe and efficient care.[15] Systems of therapeutic care include leadership, management, safety culture, processes, technology, information systems, and equipment. High-functioning teams are critical to the safe delivery of health care requiring nontechnical competency, such as communication, as well as clinical competency or clinical decision-making skills.[19]

Multi-team Patient Safety Systems in Health Care

In 2006, the U.S. Agency for Healthcare Research and Quality with the U.S. Department of Defense Military Health System released the TeamSTEPPS®—Strategies and Tools to Enhance Performance and Patient Safety programming adapting evidence-based research from other HRO sectors such as aviation, nuclear power, submarines, and the military special forces.[21] The program includes a comprehensive set of tools, strategies, and implementation methods for developing high-performing teams in the healthcare delivery setting through the building of knowledge, skills, and attitudes including team leadership, situation monitoring, mutual support, and communication. The Joint Commission estimates that as many as 70% of adverse events are the result of ineffective communication.[22] Over the last decade, TeamSTEPPS has become the most widely used teamwork improvement system in health care with specialty programming for acute care, post-acute care, and primary care teams. A key outcome of TeamSTEPPS is a multi-team system (MTS) of care (**FIGURE 1.5**). The MTS uses systems

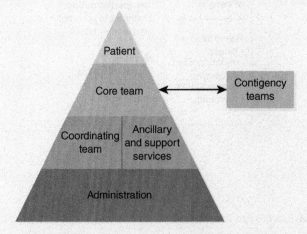

FIGURE 1.5 Multi-team System

thinking when modeling patient care systems. For instance, a labor and delivery team is the "core" team providing direct patient care to the mother, family, and unborn child. The patient includes the mother and child as well as family. The coordinating team may include a charge (supervisor) nurse and triage nurse at the time of hospital admission. Ancillary and support services can include the laboratory, pharmacy, and blood bank. Administration includes the admitting clerk, department leadership, and clinical education support staff. Contingency teams would include anesthesia should an epidural be ordered to manage pain or a rapid response team should mother or baby suffer a precipitous increase in blood pressure or decrease in oxygen levels.

This example highlights the interdependence of teams and the integrated systems of teams to ensure a safe outcome. If the baby suffers difficulty in breathing after delivery, additional teams such as the neonatal intensive care unit and respiratory therapy would need to be included in the MTS. The MTS ensures that the teams understand their roles and responsibilities as well as the roles and responsibilities of the other teams. This creates a shared mental model—one of the key outcomes of TeamSTEPPS. A shared mental model means that all teams and team members are "on the same page." Numerous TeamSTEPPS studies have shown positive systems improvements in patient safety including a decreased number of adverse events, a decrease in medication and transfusion errors, a decrease in worker safety, including needle stick injury and exposures, and a decrease in communication-related incidents.[23]

Microsystems Thinking

As high-performing clinical and service delivery teams have been strengthened using TeamSTEPPS, other systems-based improvement programming such as clinical microsystems thinking uses a grassroots building block approach to optimize the quality, safety, and costs of our healthcare delivery systems.[24] Health professionals are at the frontline of healthcare delivery—optimally positioning them to design and redesign higher-quality patient care. Clinical microsystem improvement programming uses systems thinking at the smallest systems level known as the microsystem (**FIGURE 1.6**). Surgical patients move through pre-op, operating room,

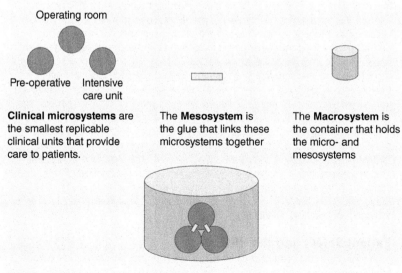

Operating room

Pre-operative   Intensive
                 care unit

Clinical microsystems are the smallest replicable clinical units that provide care to patients.

The **Mesosystem** is the glue that links these microsystems together

The **Macrosystem** is the container that holds the micro- and mesosystems

FIGURE 1.6 Clinical Microsystems Thinking

(continues)

BOX 1.4 Systems Thinking for Patient Safety   (continued)

intensive care unit or post-anesthesia care unit, and then to a surgical ward until they are discharged. The mesosystem must provide a coordinated connection between systems using MTS methods. Electronic health records and clinical decision support technology can help bridge clinical knowledge gaps between systems, while the macrosystem provides the hard structure environment, policies, equipment, personnel, and organizational culture. Clinical microsystem improvement teams must first map their current clinical practices and processes. The process mapping informs system variability, waste, and opportunities for improvement. Evidence-based research provides practical improvement options such as a checklist for central line insertion or a proven protocol for the systematic removal of Foley catheters before a patient experiences a catheter-associated urinary tract infection. Teams collect, analyze, and track performance indicators over time to ensure that new interventions are effective, enabling them to make data-driven clinical decisions with their patients.[25]

Engineering Patient Safety Systems

The University of Wisconsin introduced the Systems Engineering Initiative for Patient Safety (SEIPS) model to address the sociotechnical system (work system), processes of care, and the resultant systems outcomes (**FIGURE 1.7**).[26] Systems feedback loops are integral to system learning, adaptation, and continuous improvement. The SEIPS model builds on a successful human factor engineering framework that focuses on systems orientation (with persons central to the work system but not the single failure point) and person-centered design for patients, families, and healthcare professionals to promote higher reliability.[26]

The SEIPS model has been applied broadly to improve the reliability of patient service delivery pathways such as surgery, intensive care, and medication safety. The SEIPS model attempts to redesign healthcare systems to be more user-friendly, ergonomically efficient, and person-centered. The SEIPS model provides a framework for continuous improvement by providing the feedback loops essential to systems thinking, leading to understanding why a specific outcome (desired or undesired) occurred. The model is sensitive to unintended consequences, behavior drift or normalized deviance, and the external environment from regulators such as the Joint Commission of State Health Departments.[26]

SEIPS provides a comprehensive, systems thinking approach to patient safety, yet the model may be difficult to scale in healthcare organizations without a commitment from senior leaders, investment in safety engineering and human factors professionals, and adequate frontline resources (especially time) to engage in the endeavor of improving work. The SEIPS approach highly leverages socio-technical systems thinking to show the interactions of various work system factors such as technology, tasks, environment, organization, and people.[27] Socio-technical systems thinking is often used in patient safety investigations and retrospective root cause analysis.[27] This approach focuses on what happened and why it happened rather than who did it, allowing learning to occur based on team crisis response, identified threats, and harm management practices (**FIGURE 1.8**).

Patient Safety and the HRO

High reliability in the context of patient safety means reducing preventable serious safety events which lead to patient deaths and serious injuries. The concept of HROs for health care has developed over the last decade, focusing on attributes

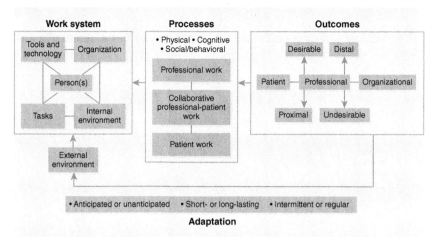

FIGURE 1.7 SEIPS Model for Patient Safety

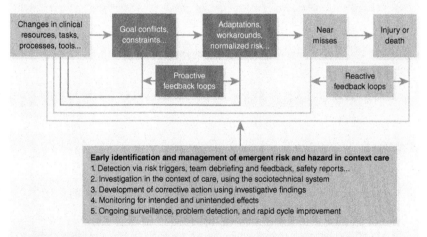

FIGURE 1.8 Socio-technical Approach to Patient Safety Performance and Learning Systems for Threat and Error Management

and principles practiced by other high-risk industries.[19] Chassin and Loeb describe an HRO model for health care built on three pillars: leadership, culture, and robust process improvement.[28] **FIGURE 1.9** demonstrates how each pillar interacts with the other and is essential to achieve higher reliability. This patient safety model combines the benefits of TeamSTEPPS (higher reliability teams) and SEIPS (higher reliability processes/systems) with leadership (higher performing leaders) to achieve high reliability outcomes.

Furthermore, Chassin and Loeb highlight the lack of systems resilience in health care—an essential component of HROs.[28] Other high-risk industries (HROs) are more sensitive to complacency, unwilling to accept unnecessary risks, and use errors as a learning opportunity. The HRO model for health care places an increased emphasis

(continues)

BOX 1.4 Systems Thinking for Patient Safety *(continued)*

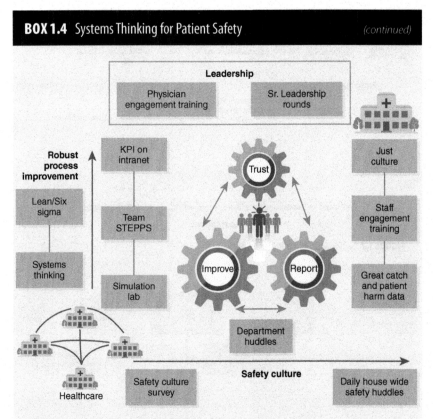

FIGURE 1.9 HRO Methods and Practices in Healthcare Organizations

on organizational culture—the beliefs, values, and norms about patient safety as well as the impact a pathological culture may have on patient safety. The challenge to adopting the HRO model is the commitment to a significant change in behaviors from the boardroom to the bedside, meaning that leaders must "walk the talk" while frontline high reliability teams must promote peer-to-peer accountability to safe practice and mutual trust regardless of rank or professional hierarchy. The HRO systems thinking is focused on a journey toward safer care—measuring organizations through maturity levels of implementation and practice while embracing safety science across the process improvement continuum.

Summary

Patient safety requires systems thinking to reduce the impact of preventable patient harm in health care. Patient safety has borrowed heavily from other high-risk industries, human factors, engineering, organizational development, and psychology to develop safer care systems designed to reduce preventable patient harm. Unfortunately, few industry drivers exist to compel health systems to adopt, implement, and sustain systems thinking approaches to patient safety, resulting sadly in pockets of safety excellence rather than widespread scalability of safe, reliable care.

References

1. von Bertalanffy L. *General Systems Theory*. New York, NY: George Braziller, Inc.; 1968.
2. Kuhn T. *The Structure of Scientific Revolutions*. Chicago, IL: University of Chicago Press; 1962.
3. Capra FC, Luisi PL. *The Systems View of Life*. Cambridge, UK: Cambridge University Press; 2014.
4. Bellinger G. Systems thinking: an operational perspective of the universe. http://www.systems -thinking.org/systhink/systhink.htm. 2004. Accessed January 4, 2018.
5. Anderson V, Johnson, L. *Systems Thinking Basics: From Concepts to Causal Loops*. Westford, MA: Pegasus Communications, Inc.; 1997.
6. Johnson JA, Stoskopf CH, Shi L. *Comparative Health Systems: Global Perspectives*. Burlington, MA: Jones and Bartlett Publishers; 2018.
7. Johnson JA, Rossow CC. *Health Organizations: Theory, Behavior, and Development*. Burlington, MA: Jones and Bartlett Publishers; 2018.
8. Taylor FW. *The Principles of Scientific Management*. New York, NY: Harper and Brothers Publishers; 1911.
9. Johnson JA, Anderson DE. *Systems Thinking for Health Organizations, Leadership, and Policy*. Austin, TX: Sentia Publishing; 2017.
10. Senge PF. *The Fifth Discipline: The Art and Practice of the Learning Organization*. New York, NY: Doubleday; 1990.
11. Hoover K, Donovan T. *The Elements of Social Scientific Thinking*. Belmont, CA: Wadsworth-Cengage Learning; 2008.
12. de Savigny D, Taghreed A. *Systems Thinking for Health Systems Strengthening*. Geneva, Switzerland: World Health Organization; 2009.
13. Skochelak SE, Hawkins RE, Lawson LE, Starr SR, Borkan JM, Gonzalo JD. *Health Systems Science*. Philadelphia, PA: Elsevier; 2017.
14. Meadows DH. *Thinking in Systems, A Primer*. White River Junction, VT: Chelsea Green Publishing; 2008.
15. Powell S, Stone R. *The Patient Survival Handbook: Avoid Being the Next Victim of Medical Error*. Alpharetta, GA: BookLogix Publishing Services; 2015.
16. Makary MA, Daniel M. Medical error-the third leading cause of death in the US. *BMJ: Br Med J*. 2016;353:i2139.
17. James JT. A new, evidence-based estimate of patient harms associated with hospital care. *J Patient Saf*. 2013;9(3):122-128.
18. Human TEI. *Building a Safer Health System*. Washington, DC: Institute of Medicine; 2000:112.
19. Powell SM. Creating a systems approach to patient safety through better teamwork. *Biomed Instrum Technol*. 2006;40(3):205-207.
20. Emanuel L, Berwick D, Conway J, et al. *What Exactly is Patient Safety?* Rockville, MD: Agency for HealthCare Quality and Research, Advance in Patient Safety; 2008.
21. King HB, Battles J, Baker DP, et al. *TeamSTEPPS™: Team Strategies and Tools to Enhance Performance and Patient Safety*. Rockville, MD: Agency for HealthCare Quality and Research; 2008.
22. Wu AW, Lipshutz AK, Pronovost PJ. Effectiveness and efficiency of root cause analysis in medicine. *JAMA* 2008;299(6):685-687.
23. Weaver SJ, Dy SM, Rosen MA. Team-training in healthcare: a narrative synthesis of the literature. *BMJ Qual Saf Health Care*. 2014:23(5):359-372.
24. Likosky DS. Clinical microsystems: a critical framework for crossing the quality chasm. *J Extra Corpor Technol*. 2014;46(1):33.
25. Nelson EC, Batalden PB, Homa K, et al. Microsystems in health care: Part 2. Creating a rich information environment. *Jt Comm J Qual Saf*. 2003;29(1):5-15.
26. Holden RJ, Carayon P, Gurses AP, et al. SEIPS 2.0: a human factors framework for studying and improving the work of healthcare professionals and patients. *Ergonomics*. 2013;56(11):1669-1686.
27. Burger C, Eaton P, Hess K, et al. System-based approach to managing patient safety in ambulatory care (and beyond). *Patient Safety and Quality Healthcare*. https://www.psqh.com /analysis/system-based-approach-managing-patient-safety-ambulatory-care-beyond/. Nov /Dec 2017. Accessed March 3, 2018.
28. Chassin MR, Loeb JM. High-reliability health care: getting there from here. *Milbank Q*. 2013;91(3):459-490.

CHAPTER 2

Systems Thinking for Health Administration and Leadership

▶ Why Health Administrators and Leaders Must Embrace Systems Thinking

Most health administrators and leaders have a basic understanding of systems thinking whether it is implied as part of CQI or part of the strategic planning process. However, the real power lies in applying systems thinking in the broader context of the health ecosystem—components of the health system that form complex sets of relationships and functions as a whole to interact with each other—and health system transformation. The current systems dynamics (i.e., regulatory, political, payment) and the current performance of the health system underscore a need to reframe challenges with systems thinking competencies—knowledge, skills, behaviors, and attributes—to create sustainable solutions. Unfortunately, many health administrators and leaders rush to quick solutions, solve the wrong problem, miss opportunities, and cling to the comfort of spheres of influence or silos blind to the malaise, dysfunctions, and opportunities throughout the ecosystem. Today's health administrators and leaders must be more adept at seeing "the forest and the trees" or connections and interdependencies of processes and phenomena within and outside the walls of their organizations. Their functional responsibilities to achieve outcomes, such as those associated with the Institute of Health Improvement's Triple Aim (e.g., population health, experience of care, and reduced cost per capita), are being challenged with the need to improve coordination of care, leverage and support social services, and increase the quality of life in the communities they serve.

If health administrators more consistently apply systems thinking, the benefits of higher reliability and better health for the community population, reduced system costs, and increased quality of life will follow. The purpose of this chapter is to illustrate why health administrators must embrace a systems approach and thinking as a critical competency. This chapter provides answers to why systems thinking is essential and recommends how to apply systems thinking. Case studies and interviews complement the need for systems thinking as a competency.

▶ Why a Systems Approach and Thinking Should Be Important

Although the U.S. health system excels in several areas, performance remains uneven regarding safety, quality, value, and health outcomes. By most reports, the United States ranks 37th in the world with regard to health outcomes. Preventable deaths due to medical errors have been a top cause of death since 2001 with minimal change. Many health administrators view this tragic statistic as normal. Furthermore, when a sector consumes upstream of 20% of the nation's gross national product, 20% of the amount is attributed to waste and inefficiency, and another 20% could have been avoided through better health, wellness, and resilience.[1,2]

The United States loses approximately 10% of its national productivity per year as a result of healthcare issues, and the nation spends nearly twice as much on health care than most other countries. Although overall health expenditures continue to grow, several studies suggest up to 30% of health expenditures are unnecessary.[1-3] The problem is not with individuals working in the health system, but with the design and operation of multiple complex systems. These health systems add unnecessary burdens to clinical workflows, cumbersome episodes of care processes, and rigid management activities. If health administrators applied a systems approach and systems thinking as a prominent competency, performance gaps could be closed.[3]

While outcomes tend to cluster around the Triple Aim, other performance measures associated with the Triple Aim include financial sustainability, safety, planning, staff satisfaction, community service, leadership development, and ethical decision-making. For purposes of discussion, three groups comprise health administrators—governing body, chief executive officer, and senior managers of respective specialty areas—referred to collectively as the "c-suite" and will be referred to as such throughout the primer.[4] These health administrators are accountable to the governing body and work to integrate the myriad of complex processes to achieve the intended outcomes.[5-8]

Health administrators must view themselves as part of a more extensive health system or as health system executives who have the resources, influence, and control to achieve their organization's mission, vision, and goals. Intuitively, health administrators understand general systems theory—concepts, framework, direction, and decisions—representing a systems approach.[9] General systems theory suggests health organizations are goal-directed, have identifiable inputs, contain work processes at all levels to convert inputs to outputs, and also have feedback loops to control the system.[9] A "systems approach" provides a logical arrangement of components to demonstrate a progression from inputs to outputs, including the community health system at large. The main elements of this arrangement are inputs (resources or money, workforce, and supplies), structure (departments, units, and sections), processes (preventive, curative, and diagnostic care), and outputs or outcomes.[10] The functional components of the U.S. health services delivery structure are, at best, a loosely coordinated system. These components can be identified using a systems framework.

To be successful, health administrators need to stop viewing the organization as a conglomerate of silos or units (i.e., planning, finance, revenue cycle, continuous quality improvement (CQI), human resource management (HRM), patient services, facilities, materials, contracting, and procurement) and think of the organization as a "system of systems" or processes, people, and resources achieving an outcome often in collaboration with the community as part of the health "ecosystem."[5-8] A systems approach applies insights to understand how elements influence the intended outcomes. Systems approach models illustrate the relationships between design, processes, or policies to produce better health and care at lower cost or greater efficiency. Systems approaches today should have applicability for issues facing health systems such as working with social, public, and non-health agencies to reduce hospital readmissions, decrease high costs associated with homelessness, and reduce STDs.[3,10-12]

As an example of a healthcare organization systems approach, the Baldrige model emphasizes management and analysis of the whole system working together in an organization to influence outcomes. The criteria represent a systems approach. Many organizations use the criteria as the basis for developing a systems perspective, achieving integration, and streamlining operations. The six system process categories must be integrated to ensure proper functioning across the organization. Successful performance should drive alignment and integration of goals and objectives across departments. This alignment ensures that measures, indicators, competencies, and knowledge guide decisions and CQI.[13] Regardless of level in the organization, applying a systems approach and using the tools of systems thinking should result in CQI results. At the same time, the Baldrige model implies that the health administrator's health services delivery roles and responsibilities begin and end at their organization's doorsteps.

Furthermore, health administrators set "invisible" tones throughout their health system by establishing the culture through words, stories, actions, and behaviors. As part of the Baldrige criteria and standards from the Joint Commission on Accreditation of Healthcare Organizations (JCAHO), health administrators must look at the "whole" system, including cultural systems such as diversity, and determine how well an individual responds (friction versus non-friction) to the organization's needs. A culture that values high reliability, quality, respect, responsibility, community service, and ethical behavior achieves their goals of better health and care.[5] To go deeper, cultural diversity encompasses a person's beliefs, values, family structure practice, and mind-set—a personal system that is part of the larger health system. Consequently, cultural, community, and environmental experiences or systems diversity supports teamwork, reengineering, empowerment, quality, and innovation in an organization. Systems diversity relates to the differences among organizations in work structure, pursuits, and perspectives—linear and nonlinear thinking. Systems diversity involves systems thinking and the ability to recognize how functions in the work environment are connected with diversity.[14] Systems diversity is an element of the systems approach. Health administrators must be cognizant of these invisible systems, so their teams can focus on translating the organization's visions and strategies into their daily practice.

However, the Baldrige model may confine organizations to their processes. Today, success depends on how well health administrators collaborate within the "walls" of their organizations AND the overall health "ecosystem." It is not an "Either/Or" proposition; it is a "Yes, And" mandate. For example, payment models such as capitation financing are driving health organizations to partner with hotels and home health agencies to coordinate care and avoid readmission penalties at lower costs.[15,16] A systems approach beyond the Baldrige model has the potential to drive systems thinking beyond the walls of a typical healthcare organization and improve the health of the entire community. For example, integrating behavioral health services with primary care, public health, and social services partners may result in improved community health outcomes and more operating capacity (i.e., appointment availability, preventive care, more time with patients) in the healthcare system, or reduced wait time in the healthcare system. By reframing our thinking beyond the Baldrige model to understand how elements operate interdependently, we can leverage additional capabilities or leverage the social determinants of health in the health ecosystem to improve health and, subsequently, net cost per capita.

Unfortunately, many health administrators fail to see "the forest and the trees" in their health system, and they tend to solve problems in a linear suboptimal manner.[5,17] These systems approaches remain underutilized and untapped throughout the health system.[3] Health administrators need to adopt the right management style and move away from a top down and silo mentality and manage sideways throughout the system. A systems approach and competency of systems thinking can help. Health administrators who align culture with environmental trends and strategic planning efforts are more likely to transform successfully. Health administrators must be able to transcend organizational boundaries in today's health environment—that is, move beyond the Baldrige model. Health administrators must be capable of reframing their goals and organizational boundaries to move their organizations forward in a strategic direction.[18] Health organizations that embrace the tenants of complex adaptive health systems to anticipate growth in the strategic community partnerships will position themselves to thrive in an era of complexity. Health administrators with a systems thinking mind-set will form new partnerships as a means to succeed.[19]

Specifically, health administrators must connect the parts of the whole system at the organization and operations levels. To get the complete picture, health administrators need an in-depth knowledge of the entire organization, the parts, and the impact of each component on one another. Health administrators must see the chain reactions of their decisions and nondecisions or unintended consequences. Health administrators need to understand the adaptive nature of systems. As dynamic entities, systems adjust to changes imposed on them—often with unpredictable results. Health administrators, therefore, need to know how the actions they take in any one part of the system—at the organizational or operational levels—will cascade down to affect the whole.

▶ Why Systems Thinking Must Be Part of Organizational Development and Culture

While the majority of health administrators understand their mission, vision, goals, and policies, understanding and influencing whole systems may require reframing their approaches to conflict and problem-solving. There are silos or "subsystems" at work representing functions such as financial management, population health, strategic management, marketing, HRM, and quality improvement. Identifying the connections, factors, and influences between these functions may not be as apparent as it relates to producing better value.

Understanding and anticipating how the whole system is intended to function actually works, and foreseeing how it may buckle can elude the most adept health administrators. The challenge is realizing that for every official organization, there is an invisible organization or culture. The invisible organization is where all the politics, trust, hopes, ambitions, greed, favors, and power struggles reside. The system can confuse, overpower, block, and fail health administrators. However, health administrators can fail the system.[20] For example, organizational conflict is examined using possible patterns, intertwining sequences, roles, relationships, and the processing of information—a systems thinking approach. Occurrences such as these impose considerable change, thus producing conflict.[5] At the same time, conflict is healthy, especially when divergent views are utilized. These complex views illustrate conflict as a dynamic: escalating and de-escalating, changing form, spreading into new groups, and having the ability to pass these views from generation to generation.[14] Future health administrators with systems thinker's competencies will be able to leverage resources in the organizations and community for better effect.

While conflict may be healthy, unchecked conflict may only be the tip of the iceberg, driving costly mistakes, poor morale, incivility, and turnover. As an example, reducing conflict such as incivility should be viewed in the context of organizational leadership system. Many view incidents of incivility as a data point to be quickly solved (many times ignored) and referred to the HRM resolution. While HRM is a function, their responsibilities permeate the whole organization and do not absolve supervisors of their responsibilities. HRM systems are composed of subsystems (hire, orientation, promotion, discipline, and pay) that comprise several inputs (e.g., policies, processes, practices, training, supervisors, and employees) and may be broken down into additional subsystems.[20] Some view HRM as having clear boundaries (closed) and responsibilities while their environment (open) drives them to work more closely with supervisors. However, an open systems perspective—proper leadership, supportive culture, and collaborative approaches—should be more familiar and realistic.[20]

In the example of incivility, health administrators adept at systems thinking would begin examining the organization's culture (human and organizational dynamics at work), looking for friction points or patterns between management systems, and recognizing how they themselves contribute to incivility. In the case of incivility, systems thinkers would view the organization in the context of the environment followed by understanding, analyzing, and talking about the design of an effective supervisory development program that focuses on working together and applying the skills of proper supervision.[20] For example, some managers view HRM as the first stop for hiring and the last stop for firing. Reducing incivility goes beyond the HRM department. To implement an effective work relations program, organizational readiness—openness, visibility, and transparency—is necessary. Health administrators who take a "holistic" approach to reducing adverse HRM actions and improve interdepartmental relations by solving the crisis with a silver bullet solution such as letters of admonishment are short term.

An organization as an entity can suffer systemic failure. Administrative systems operate alongside each other in a formal hierarchy. HRM includes supervision, pay, and documentation. However, the cultural dynamics such as noneffective supervision may impact incivility.[20] Failure occurs if the whole system elements are not working together for overall success.[20] Factors contributing to incivility may include a weak system-wide understanding of the goals, a flawed design of the process, inadequate feedback, poor cooperation, and lack of accountability.[20] In many cases, health administrators look the other way hoping the issue goes away only to find reduced unit morale, decreased personal credibility, and increasing incidents.

Reducing civility equates to an applied systems approach aligned with the organization's goals. Examples include group or team-level goal-setting across department silos, leader development, incentives, communication, reviews, rewards, and accountability. As a system, the aim is to focus on what binds individual systems rather than functional or departmental performance.[20] Implementing and enforcing policies, conducting "work relations" training and organizational climate surveys, and establishing anonymous reporting systems for detecting unprofessional behavior are examples of cultural subsystems at work. Interventions must be conducted within the context of the staff's well-being with adequate resources to support individuals whose behavior is caused or influenced by physical or mental pathologies. The approach may include "safe zones" for employees to provide feedback or gather feedback from staff, patients, and families who may experience intimidating or disruptive behavior. As a preventive and maintenance approach, reducing incivility should also include a monitoring system with regular surveys, focus groups, peer and team member evaluations, or other methods that will help uncover pockets and patterns of potentially intimidating or disruptive behaviors.[5]

Health administrators and supervisors should adopt personalized interventions, enablers, and preventive systems approaches. *System interventions* such as progressive feedback include discipline to build trust for future anonymous reporting and places accountability on rehabilitating the offending individual. System enablers such as mediators and coaches with professional dispute resolution skills may be needed. *System prevention* such as random rounding and informal "cup of coffee" conversations with staff, supervisors, and peers reinforces the health administrators' commitment to supporting nonconfrontational interactions between individuals, groups, or units.

Whether a health administrator, nurse manager, or materials management supervisor, systems thinking is a competency to produce a better understanding of a system by examining the linkages and interactions between the components that comprise the entirety of that defined system.[20] As stewards of the system, health administrators are responsible for thinking about the impact of proposed changes on the system, its patients, families, and other takeovers today and in the future. Solving problems with systems thinking begins and ends with an understanding of how the whole system interacts with the environment and how its parts interact to achieve a purpose.

Systems thinking helps health administrators understand why something works as it does.[21] While this illustrative case discusses HRM and incivility, health administrators must integrate the complex processes of their organization into a cohesive system to produce outcomes on razor-thin profit margins. Systems thinking is central to uncovering dysfunctions, identifying opportunities to improve, developing and testing solutions, and implementing changes to the whole system. Health administrators who are adept at systems thinking know that making changes to a small part of a system can lead to the organization's suboptimization and unintended consequences for the more extensive system.

▶ Why Systems Thinking Enhances Performance Improvement and Operations

To create a culture of reliability, health administrators must sustain a focus on the bigger picture. Complex health systems have interacting components working in expected and unexpected ways. Health administrators should plan, implement, and improve interactions by actively listening and asking difficult questions while maintaining an eye on the relationships between the parts of their system. Theories about high reliability and human factors can teach us how to build more reliable processes and services throughout the health system. A small change in one part of the system, such as standardized medical supplies versus personal preferences, can produce a significant effect elsewhere. Understanding the human–system interface allows us to improve the design of error-proof systems and processes. Having high reliability enables us to understand the whole system as visible and invisible parts, rather than the results of actions and handoffs. Health administrators must employ pervasive "mindfulness" for unanticipated changes and performance by applying systems thinking in the management of an organization.[22,23]

Systems thinking enables whole system performance in the context of performance improvement (PI) initiatives. If systems are defined informally as the collection of subsystems that share performance to achieve an outcome, then the systems approach provides a framework and systems thinking consists of assessing the interconnections, interdependencies, and relationships among subsystems. Health administrators must be capable of focusing on the past, including suspending judgment and seeking out the interrelatedness of how inputs and outputs are created and achieving sustainable solutions by combining systems thinking and PI for a more significant impact. While PI is the interplay of parts to produce higher productivity and economy of operations, systems thinking broadens the potential to produce higher reliability and staff satisfaction throughout the system. Systems thinking and PI should complement each other to be effective. Systems thinking looks for patterns in the relationships among processes, isolating causes and effects of dysfunctional processes, and allows players to generate creative solutions. PI seeks to improve the system with facts and process improvement activities.[13]

Systems thinking should improve operations. Another perspective on the systems approach involves operations research (OR). OR quickly became known for incorporating scientific processes into decision-making. A systems approach refers to how OR studies underlying behavior and structure of the systems—or interrelated processes, events, and activities—define most problems. For example, a systems approach and OR technique can help health administrators understand capacity constraints and scope of end-to-end patient flows using models and simulation.[24] Both systems thinking and OR can ensure that resources are available in a hospital setting when patients need them by understanding the dynamics and complexities of the processes of care and subsystem support (i.e., revenue cycle and coding, materials management and coding). The approach would include examining how patients enter and move through the hospital, from initial admission, through the different ancillary units, until their discharge. Importantly, these processes must include scheduled cases (such as elective surgeries) and unscheduled cases (such as emergency admissions), as both contribute to variability in the hospital census. The patient data are analyzed using mathematical models and the results are applied to adjust hospital processes, such as the daily operating room schedule, and lower variability in the flow of patients to different hospital units.[3]

Systems thinking and an OR approach recognize relationships exist between the environment and internal processes and aim to analyze and develop models for simulating options. For example, Cincinnati Children's Hospital was able to improve quality while simultaneously increasing surgical volume by 7% annually for 2 years without adding staff or increasing the number of hospital beds.[3] Similar results have been noted at the Mayo Clinic in Florida, which implemented this methodology and was able to increase surgical volumes by 4% while decreasing variability by 20%, reducing staff turnover by 40%, and reducing overtime staffing by 30%.[3] When systems are modeled, they can then be manipulated in various ways to estimate the effects of changing policies or decisions. Therefore, when applied to management, a combined OR and a systems approach can be a powerful means for improving results or making better informed decisions.[24]

To summarize, combining PI and OR with systems thinking produces a highly effective approach for managing organizations at the organizational level. Various divisions, units, and teams—the components—of a large organization interact more effectively. Health administrators need to maintain a "whole-system" perspective if they aim to maximize organizational performance. From a healthcare administrator's perspective, systems thinking requires a genuine understanding of both sides of the demand and supply equation in the context of a system. Health administrators must explore how friction causes bottlenecks. Health administrators must seek out and find the visible and invisible constraints such as policies on systems diversity. While PI and OR measure peaks, valleys, and troughs, health administrators must assess systems for subtle effects such as how external factors are affecting the work environment and how much demand is a function of lack of resource capacity.

The discussion illustrates why health administrators must embrace systems thinking. Health administrators must perceive themselves as health system executives and undertake a systematic approach to transforming health systems. For many years, JCAHO standards reinforced stovepipes: "Management," "Governance," "Medical Staff," and "Nursing Services." Each department had a set of standards. Rather than think about their organization as departments, health administrators must think in terms of systems—combination of processes, people and resources working across departments—to see interconnections between whole systems. Applying systems thinking is needed to transform today's health system or generate sustainable solutions.[5]

Sustainable solutions depend on systems thinking or recognizing the organization as a system to produce outcomes. Health administrators adept at systems thinking understand the environment and how culture impacts the system's performance. An organization's culture reflects the beliefs, attitudes, and priorities of the staff throughout the organization. For example, if the CEO focuses only on financial sustainability, the system will "spiral" downstream impacting safety, staff satisfaction, and poor care.[5] As the HRM examples illustrate, issues such as incivility result from problems in the system and inattention.[25]

Systems approaches can be useful at all levels of the health system with systems thinking tools in the context of organization development, medical supply chains flow, or community health systems integration. These tools include soft systems and production methods to help organizations continuously improve the whole system. Spreading these systems principles more broadly requires additional education and training.[3] Unfortunately, a systems approach and systems thinking is not well defined and varies from specialty to specialty. For example, the Health Leadership Alliance (HLA) comprising specialties of administration, nursing, finance, and physician health administrators pays minimal attention to systems thinking, yet the skills are embedded in most of the functional competency areas.[6-8]

▶ Why Systems Thinking Should be a Recognized Competency

As health systems are being transformed, so are competencies—knowledge, skills, behaviors, and attributes—of health administrators. The current models of health leadership, born in the industrial age, are no longer adequate for a complex knowledge-based economy, especially in the health sector. Stand-alone health institutions are giving way to integrated information-based health systems and accountable care. This trend is driving the need for partnering throughout the health ecosystem. To improve whole systems, health administrators must pay attention to the parts and apply the tools. Linear thinking and stovepipe mentalities must be replaced by a systems approach and systems thinking as a way and means to create a desired future.[26]

▶ Lack of Systems Thinking in Health Administration Education and Training Programs

Health organization ecosystems represent a complex web of relationships, processes, and infrastructures where teams operate. For today's health administrators, a systems approach and systems thinking must be a prominent competency. A systems approach may be at odds with others who do not think in long-term, nonlinear, cause and effect, and circular ways. Systems thinking considers the "whole" system and relationships among systems and places less emphasis on the structure. Health administrators accustomed to working within their sphere of influence must work in informal networks and across organization boundaries to leverage capabilities in the communities.

The public health community has formally recognized systems thinking as a competency. Health administrators should learn from them. Public health administrators acknowledge systems thinking as an integral competency.[11,27] The health administrators' challenge becomes how to apply a systems approach, work collaboratively, and better understand the problem, so solutions become more comprehensive and improve their population's health in the health ecosystem.[28,29]

While administrative or departmental groupings are interconnected and interdependent and impact others internally or externally throughout the system, systems thinking is not prevalent in health administration activities or part of educational and leader development programs. Health administrators would benefit from systems thinking education and training for several reasons. First, familiarity with systems thinking concepts and tools is available, yet many health administrators do not have the basic skills. When health ecosystem thrives, it means the participants have developed patterns of behavior that streamline the flow of knowledge, nurture talent, and optimize the use of resources throughout the system.

Second, personal preferences affect the use of systems thinking. These preferences stem from style, experiences, and education. A lack of systems thinking can cause health administrators to focus too narrowly on quick fixes in deference to sustainable solutions. This "silo" mentality is created by health administrators who do not see "the forest and trees." They must reframe more broadly their challenges. Instead, health administrators attempt to achieve optimal functioning within defined boundaries in the department or organization. For example, administrators may be obsessed with eliminating sexually transmitted diseases (STDs) workload when a long-term solution may be engaging in community partnerships to implement school education and social marketing campaigns to reduce STDs at the source.

Third, the health education standards are replete with references to systems thinking, but they do not delineate the concepts and tools in the context of health administration nor do they become part of the curricula. Because health administrators set the direction for organizations, flows of ideas up and down departments or teams become stifled and traditional organizational boundaries "box in" their thinking. For many health administrators, acquiring a broader perspective of the system, understanding the causes and effects of the upstream (leveraging capabilities and positivity) or downstream (depletion of resources and negativity) spirals, and influencing factors related to processes, and removing barriers do not come easily to many. The root cause is lacking an understanding of systems thinking as well as lacking the potential to generate sustainable solutions. This root cause extends into how many health administrators are improperly educated, trained, and mentored or how many graduate programs are offered without systems thinking fundamentals.

Finally, systems thinking has not been formalized as a prominent competency. By becoming more aware of the concepts and tools, systems thinking applications leading to sustainable solutions will falter. Incorporating systems thinking into academic and leader development curricula will expand awareness to bolster the confidence of new learners. For example, the purpose of the Association of University Programs in Health Administration (AUPHA) Body of Knowledge (BOK) for Health Management and Policy provides healthcare administration knowledge-based standards and content students should learn. The BOK presents a heavy orientation toward organizational behavior, quality improvement, financial management, strategic planning, and marketing.[6-8] **TABLE 2.1** provides a crosswalk of selected AUPHA BOK domain and knowledge areas and presents examples regarding how systems thinking must be more prominent in education and training programs and leader development activities.[30]

To be successful in complex environments, health administrators should become systems thinkers. Systems thinkers are consciously aware that everything is connected to everything else. The apparent problems plaguing an organization may be symptoms rather than causes.[28,29] Acting as change agents for the organization requires mastering the techniques of systems thinking and looking at the organization systemically. For example, root cause analysis (RCA) and systems integration, a form of systems thinking, have grown in recent years to encompass a higher systems perspective. RCA has evolved into a highly effective systems approach to dive deeply into a complicated process to uncover multiple layers of causes and effects and interconnections. One familiar concept is the Swiss Cheese Model—how multiple systems and processes perpetuate preventable patient errors and death and not just one system or individual. Thus, one-dimensional reviews of failure points—human performance, relations, and equipment—underlie why problems in numerous interconnected processes require systems thinking.[31]

TABLE 2.1 Crosswalk of Selected AUPHA BOK Knowledge Areas and Examples[30]

AUPHA BOK Domain	Applications Using Systems Approaches Principles
Theoretical and Methodological Foundations: Organizational Behavior Management Theory Epidemiology Economics	Organizational Behavior—Learning is a nonlinear process. Focusing on the established hierarchy of scientific evidence as a basis for decision-making may not accommodate the dynamics of the environment. There is a need to bridge the gap between adherence and adaptation based on experience. Application: Reducing incivility in an organization as a systems approach.
What We Offer and How We Are Organized: Health Systems Hospitals Long-Term Care Medical Group Practice Public Health System	Health Systems—Emphases on interdependence and process interfaces beyond the walls of any health organizations are blurring. Understanding causes and effects between systems results in sustainable solutions. Application: Attention to handoffs between connected processes, including administrative processes, and at the point of care and upon discharge to other health settings such as home or telehealth services is crucial.
How We Manage: Health Administrators Organizational Structure and Governance Ethics Financial Management Information Technology Strategic Planning Marketing Health Insurance Human Resources Quality and Patient Safety	Strategic Planning—The system's processes must be centered on the right outcome—the patient, value (better health and volume) over volume, and community. Health care is complex involving multiple participants within and outside the organization, sometimes spiraling into nonvalued added activities. Application: Help solve the community's homelessness problem and their high costs of care. Integrate social workers and resources to establish community health centers for referral and less expensive outpatient care. 　Human Resources—Identify archetypes and thinking regarding circles and feedback loops (balancing and reinforcing) to identify the actual causes and effects of a process, policy, or barrier. Application: Nurse managers are critical to meeting strategic goals; however, shifting burdens (archetype) goes unchecked too often. Their expanding workload diverts attention. Solution? Empower more nurse managers as "approvers" rather than "doers," create time off buffer zones, and minimize time by eliminating insidious tasks best handled by others.

(continues)

TABLE 2.1 Crosswalk of Selected AUPHA BOK Knowledge Areas and Examples[30]   *(continued)*

AUPHA BOK Domain	Applications Using Systems Approaches Principles
External Factors: Health Policy Healthcare Law Diversity Global Healthcare Management	Health Policy—System excellence throughout the healthcare "ecosystem" is created by the reliable delivery of established best practices within and outside the health system. Policies aimed at prevention, integration, and transparency ensure participation and minimize "silver bullet" solutions. Application: Solving the substance abuse crisis requires community-wide interventions. The complexity of the substance abuse crisis requires multiple actors and stakeholders to understand the depth of the problem, so sustainable solutions can be implemented at community state and federal levels.

Adapted from the Association of University Programs in Health Administration (AUPHA) / Body of Knowledge (BOK) for Health Management and Policy.

Due to systems dynamics and innovation, organizations are continually adapting to other systems. One way to put systems thinking into practice is to think in terms of integration and interoperability of complex information and technology systems (IM/IT).[28,29] An example of complexity and a case in point are systems integration of pharmacies. Most pharmacies have dozens of interrelated systems: robots that pick, cabinets that dispense, procurement systems that order, carousels that store, pricing systems, and retail charging systems. Integrating all of these systems—from the point of order through administration, including synchronization of other systems, from computerized physician order entry systems to electronic medical records to patient billing—is required to ensure information flows quickly and accurately. Such systems integration requires systems thinking to understand the interdependencies beyond the IM/IT department, so reliability, buy-in, and early detection of problems become standard practice.[24] A systems approach allows health administrators to analyze logically the dimension of the problem.

However, applying systems thinking is not a prominent competency in health administration. For example, the American Healthcare Executives (ACHE) Competencies Assessment Tool offers an instrument for healthcare executives to use in assessing their expertise. It is based on the HLA model. *Systems thinking, systems theory,* and *champion systems thinking* are listed under Business Skills and General Management, while other HLA members such as the American Organization of Nurse Executives list systems thinking under leadership competencies.[6-8,32] Also, AUPHA's BOK supports the development of competencies in accreditation organizations such as the Commission on Accreditation of Healthcare Management Education and associations such as the ACHE and leader development programs.[6-8] **TABLE 2.2** provides a crosswalk of the ACHE competencies, systems thinking competencies, and possible applications.

TABLE 2.2 Crosswalk of ACHE Competencies and Systems Thinking Competency Examples[6]

2018 ACHE Competency Categories	Applications Involving Systems Thinking Concepts and Tools
Health Administration: Inspire individual and organizational excellence, create a shared vision and successfully manage change to attain the organization's strategic ends and successful performance. Health administrators intersect with each of the other four domains.	Health Administrators' Skills and Behavior—Use a top-down and bottom-up process to involve people who know the system best—frontline staff and service users. Communicating Vision and Managing Change—Due to the aging population and complex care costs, cancer care costs are projected to be $200 billion by 2020. At the same time, healthcare organizations are experiencing increased margin pressures and risks, mergers, and heightened consumerism. In response, cancer programs need to double down on reducing care variation and decreasing costs while improving quality.
Communication and Relationship Management: Ability to communicate clearly and concisely with internal and external customers; establish and maintain relationships; facilitate constructive interactions with individuals and groups.	Facilitation and Negotiation—Episodic payment is increasing in prevalence across the healthcare industry. A variety of payment models, including bundled payments, aim to lower the cost of care and improve care quality across the continuum. To succeed under episodic payments, post-acute providers must emerge as post-discharge solutions, representing a critical link between the hospital and the community.
Professionalism: Align personal and organizational conduct with ethical and professional standards that include a responsibility to the patient and community, service orientation, and commitment to lifelong learning and improvement.	Professional Development and Lifelong Learning—Learning about the Internet of Things (IoT) (e.g., low-cost/power computing, communications and sensors; wearables, smart homes, and smart vehicles, driverless ambulances, early warning sensors, and drones), possibilities (predict adverse events, e.g., fall risks and changes in routine), improve care plan adherence (e.g., smart medication dispensers), and streamline processes and the challenges (integration, interoperability immaturity, security, privacy, managing data, and user familiarity).

(continues)

TABLE 2.2 Crosswalk of ACHE Competencies and Systems Thinking Competency Examples[6]   *(continued)*

2018 ACHE Competency Categories	Applications Involving Systems Thinking Concepts and Tools
Knowledge of Healthcare Environment: Understanding of the healthcare system and the environment in which healthcare managers and providers function.	Patient's Perspective—Regularly walk through how the patient navigates the system. If not completed, it will be impossible to generate a map of the system and identify potential failure points. Healthcare Systems and Organizations—Regularly map user experiences; make the map available to all who need it. Process-mapping should produce shared knowledge about the causes and effects on the way a system is configured and how performance is influenced by the design—current and future—for everyone involved in improving the system.
Business Skills and Knowledge: Ability to apply business principles, including systems thinking, to the healthcare environment.	Organizational Dynamics, Strategic Planning, and Marketing—3D printing has footholds in the healthcare industry (e.g., hearing aids and dentistry), but expectations have grown due to the value of "printing anything" from vital organs to a house. The enthusiasm is justified; technology has the potential to allow healthcare organizations (and eventually patients) to design and produce cheaply and efficiently products on demand. Financial Management—With increasing patient consumerism, hospital–physician integration, and evolving payer priorities, an end-to-end focus on the revenue cycle from the clinician, ancillary, patient, and IT perspective is required to achieve performance visibility, efficiency, and accountability.

Adapted from the ACHE Competencies Assessment Tool and Health Leadership Alliance Competency categories.

Systems thinking must become a critical skill. Functions within organizations are increasingly interconnected and interdependent. The examples described illustrate why a systems approach must be more prominent in health administration education, leader development activities, and real-world applications. While RCA, a form of systems analysis and systems integration, attempts to overcome linear thinking, health administrators must look for opportunities to transform whole systems and not just parts of the systems.[29]

Complex situations and dynamics are more common. If a health administrator is involved in change-oriented activities, mastery of systems thinking is paramount. Health administrators will be more adept at recognizing the interconnectedness of their organization and communities. Nonetheless, many health administrators and managers regularly rely on linear thinking, with its sequential, short-term focus on individual parts, thus creating more complications and frustrating those who use systems thinking.[33]

As an example, systems thinking principles can be applied to improve the revenue cycle and clinical operations. In 2012, two-thirds of hospitals said they planned to replace or upgrade their revenue cycle management systems within 24 months. A similar survey in 2015 found 28% of CFOs had not fully upgraded their systems, and 88% of CFO respondents believed their system needed to be replaced. Rather than take an incremental approach, such as the transition to International Classification of Diseases (ICD)-10 and interface with the electronic health records, a systems approach would be wise.[34,35] Health administrators thinking of updating their revenue cycle management process should consider a systems approach. Reframing the approach concerning the whole systems and interfaces—healthcare teams and process, patient and family, finance and IT offices, and insurance carriers—should lead health administrators to consider integrating clinical documentation, revenue cycle management systems, and the patient experience as a system.

For several reasons, focusing on integration, satisfaction levels, clinical care alignment, and planning and education of the revenue cycle and clinical operations system—and not the cycle itself within the department—will result in increased clinical and financial effectiveness.[36] First, one of the most frustrating aspects of health care for patients is dealing with an insurer and provider to figure out why a claim was denied. The system is convoluted and difficult to navigate, and the rules are vague. No one is empowered to assess the end-to-end across the whole process, and no one is incentivized to fix it.[37] A walk-through of how a patient navigates the whole system revenue and clinical operation may uncover gaps between parts of the system and what happens to a charge or lost charge (coding process) as it moves through the system.

Second, satisfaction levels and lost revenue associated with the denial process must be assessed. From a systems thinking perspective, denials are costly for healthcare organizations regarding reputation loss, frustration, and rework. The American Academy of Family Physicians, Government Accountability Office, and other organizations report denial rates ranging between 10% and 25%. For those providers, one of every five medical claims must be reworked or appealed. Success rates vary from 55% to 98%, depending on the management team's capabilities.[34] When all else fails, write-offs can range from 1% to 5% of net patient revenue. For an average 300-bed hospital, 1% can mean $2 million to $3 million a year.[34,37,38] As part of the revenue cycle process, the causes and effects must be assessed from multiple perspectives. By looking for ways to minimize the cost of denials, the process must start at the documentation stage, apply analytics, work to prevent the frustration, and rework coding assignments earlier.[37]

Third, there should be alignment of financial and clinical workflows to consider clinical workflows, in addition to charge capture workflows. Nursing and physician workflows should be assessed and incorporated into the organizational goal. The most critical part of revamping revenue cycle management is realizing that it is not about installing software upgrades or a start-to-finish project but that it involves an ongoing iterative systems thinking process.[36]

Finally, rather than think only about software updates, a systems thinking approach should drive health administrators to form a project management team that understands technology, understands the management system, and understands financial and clinical workflows to dive into an RCA and determine how the whole revenue cycle could be improved.[36] Planning and education should be part of the organization's culture to include how to use the application, understand new workflows such as bedside verification for medication, explain why certain documentation parameters are required, and change management, so the entire organization understands the relationships among the parts.

The revenue cycle example illustrates why systems thinking as a competency should be more prominent. The importance of understanding the intersections within their scope of responsibility and throughout the system is essential. The interface between the elements of a system is where much of the challenge and work effectiveness occur.

If health administrators are responsible for orchestrating and managing the components of the system, the application of systems thinking should drive health administrators to develop, test, and implement changes to a system. Making fundamental changes to a small part of a system can lead to suboptimization and unintended consequences for the broader system when the impacts of these changes are not considered and understood. Increasing education, training, and experience is a beginning, and establishing competencies is the first step.

▶ How Systems Thinking Competencies Should Be More Prevalent in Health Administration

Health administrators know their organizations are complex and chaotic. However, they must keep an eye on the larger picture and find the patterns that are occurring or about to occur and make the necessary adjustments at the appropriate time.[26] Multiple opportunities present themselves to apply a systems approach to issues such as accountable care organizations incentives and penalties, leveraging community health resources, and generating higher patient safety reliability. Case studies on systems approaches should be spread more broadly, especially in integrating health systems.[3] Many resources and examples exist to enhance learning and practice systems thinking.[28,33] It begins with competency identification followed by education, training, and experience in the health administration's functional knowledge and competencies.

From a health administration perspective, application of a systems approach should be the ability to lead teams to benefit the entire organization. Health administrators must be able to seek out, understand, and communicate how the "whole" system contributes to the desired outcomes within and outside the organization. Otherwise, the same dysfunctions will persist. For healthcare administrators, this means not only focusing on the goals within their sphere of influence but also using their influence to benefit the entire system. Health administrators must be able to collaborate across the health "ecosystem" with clinicians and public health officials, helping agencies and local businesses improve health and productivity.

Systems thinking requires adaptive leadership. Health administrators must see beyond their direct responsibilities within and outside the organization. Systems thinking is about whole systems, patterns, and opportunities as they emerge, and connecting the dots to create sustainable solutions. As health administrators gain skills and confidence in systems thinking practices, they will be tempted to see every organizational problem as a systems issue.[33,39] This is in contrast to a separate or linear technical issue—where the problem is understood, and the solution is known. They must learn to lead with a big-picture view and address causes to problems that exist within the system, instead of fixing symptoms regardless of the level of work. They must train themselves to look for and recognize the complex interrelationship between multiple variables contributing to a problem and the desired outcome.

Systems thinking should drive health administrators, especially senior health administrators, to develop critical success factors and insist on sustainable solutions that are good for the organization and, in many cases, the communities they serve. Examples of critical success factors associated with a systems approach to health include reimbursement systems that reward value and outcomes via partnering, a supportive culture and organization to produce high reliability, cross-boundary leadership to improve coordination of care, and expanding digital infrastructure to reach patients in the community or region. Identifying systems thinking competencies and embedding those competencies in education and training and leader development programs is a must-do can't-fail proposition. **TABLE 2.3** is a distillation of suggested systems thinking competencies for health administrators and leaders from notable authors and practitioners.[26,28,29,33,40-52]

TABLE 2.3 Systems Thinking Competencies for Health Administrators and Leaders

Traditional versus Systems Thinking	Summary and Example
Micro → Macro View	Envisions the Big Picture, Develops and Communicates Vision—Senses signals; sees the future. Develops aspirational vision, strategy, plans, and capabilities to meet the needs of customers, suppliers, and stakeholders. Seeks out and understands the health (e.g., public and community) and healthcare system interrelationships within the system at any level. Focuses on the health system interconnections first, then the relationships, and then the causes and effects of the relationships. Proactively engages followers, teams, partners, and stakeholders to aspire to a greater vision with inter- and intrapersonal communication or outreach. Makes vision clear, meaningful, and understandable.
Disconnected → Connected Networks	Assumes Chaos and Dynamics and Leads Change—Assesses connections, disconnections, and interdependencies in a dynamic heath system that is loosely networked; elements such as social determinants of health are related, interact, and adapt to conditions in the environment in order to thrive. Holds the tension of paradox and ambiguity to understand the dynamics of a system before acting or making decisions prematurely. Seeks out opportunities to leverage better health and reliability. Sets the tone, pace, and example to lead change. Aligns and integrates concepts, strategy, capabilities, organizations, and processes into common practice and culture.

(continues)

TABLE 2.3 Systems Thinking Competencies for Health Administrators and Leaders   *(continued)*

Traditional versus Systems Thinking	Summary and Example
Silos → Patterns in Network	Actively Listens and Searches for Emerging Patterns or Themes in Dynamic Environments—Suspends judgment; objectively understands cause-and-effect relationships across systems (e.g., departments or organizations); seeks out data, relationships, stories, and hunches on issues between systems (inter and intra). Engages in and understands the concerns and needs of individuals and teams; conveys empathy to uncover possibilities; and provides support by removing barriers.
Analysis → Synthesis	Critical Thinker—Applies agile thinking to anticipate or find opportunity in complex, uncertain, and ambiguous (VUCA) situations. Synthesizes trends and behavior over time. Analyzes, then synthesizes changes in data, behavior, and relationships as part of the natural systems dynamics, operations, or volatility of an uncertain environment. Uses adaptive thinking to solve problems or shift momentum to apply sustainable solutions.
Single → Integrated Viewpoints	Integrates Multiple Viewpoints and Applies Ethics—Explores how different mental models create different views of the future. Looks at multiple perspectives of an issue from various stakeholders and processes owner viewpoints. If required, changes perspective to see other points of view within a system once a view of the whole system is complete. Serves as a role model for unwavering ethical decision-making and respect for autonomy, non-maleficence, beneficence, and justice.
Surface → Deep Dive	Takes Deep Dives to Challenge Assumptions and Status Quo—Is comfortable with questioning other's and self's assumptions. Actively listens to go beyond the surface to understand deeper issues: beliefs, values, emotions, facts or lack of facts, and thinking (fixed or silo) about how the world works (mental models) or how an existing problem should be solved. Develops new ideas, concepts, sustainable solutions, and better processes.
Ripple → Multiple Ripples	Expect Second- and Third-Order Effects—Anticipates the ripple effects of their actions and the impact on the organizational culture. To do so, health administrators must involve critical internal and external stakeholders in the decisions that have widespread impact to achieve sustainable results. Looks ahead and anticipates not only the immediate results of actions but also the second- and third-order effects throughout the system.

Quick Fix → Leverage System	<u>Lifelong Learner Who Seeks, Leverages, Uses, Generates, and Shares Knowledge</u>—Constantly applies leverage points in a complex system. Is proactive and flexible to address bottlenecks, crazy makers, and constraints. Is mindful of identifying leverage points within systems that result in positive change and incremental performance improvements before they become dysfunctional. Looks for small actions or "whispers" that can make significant differences. Uses systems understanding to determine what small actions can produce high-leverage sustainable results rather than quick fixes.
Spills → Flow	<u>Develops Leaders and Teams of Leaders</u>—Minimizes the impacts (non-flows or spillover) of accumulation of stocks over time: Pays attention to potential non- and problematic flows and spillover of resources and valuable and nonvaluable processes that build up (or deplete) over time and contribute (or do not contribute) to planned flows or support goals and objectives. Looks for deeper causes and effects throughout the system. Coaches, guides, and mentors leaders and teams. Encourages self-development and intrinsic motivation. Gives constructive feedback. Assures education and training opportunities.
Event → Loops and Circles	<u>Applies Systems Approach</u>—Assesses situations systematically; understands interconnections between systems and processes to develop strategy, solve problems, and make complex decisions. Engages in loop or circular thinking. Looks for interconnected and interdependent issues. Perceives connections between multiple issues, handoffs, or whole organizations within the health ecosystem.
Incident → Systemic Causes and Effects	<u>Empowers Others to Think Critically About Cause and Effect, Not Positions</u>—It is not just about correlation and static data points. Looks beyond primary connections using circular thinking to understand the dynamic relationship between the connected parts. Looks for the virtuous positive and vicious negative spirals or patterns that impact the entire system and design systems to naturally generate sustainable results.
Snapshots → Insights	<u>Serves as a Steward of Resources</u>—Checks results and changes in actions to achieve insight. Constantly assesses progress with a systemic view of the whole system. Assesses for improvement opportunities using benchmarks, exemplars, and innovative ideas. Uses errors and setbacks as a means to learn and adjust. Judiciously allocates and aligns resources (i.e., money, personnel, information, equipment, infrastructure, and environment) with strategy efficiently and effectively from a systems perspective.

(continues)

TABLE 2.3 Systems Thinking Competencies for Health Administrators and Leaders   *(continued)*

Traditional versus Systems Thinking	Summary and Example
Structure → Network of Processes	Empowers Others—Shares leadership collectively. Knows structural issues cause change. Builds, aligns, and sustains diverse teams of leaders to achieve the vision and outcomes. Measures progress and results systemically. Is careful not to pin the blame on a specific person. Understands and explains to others that the complexities within the system may take a longer time to correct. Looks for the virtuous positive and vicious negative spirals or patterns that impact the entire system and designs systems to generate sustainable results naturally.
Insulation → Collaboration Across Boundaries	Collaborates Across Internal and External Boundaries—Understands boundaries are arbitrary. Checks for consistency of understanding about where boundaries are drawn. Collaborates across boundaries to leverage systems and create synergy. Builds mutually beneficial relationships and common goals within and across organizations. Partners with networks and communities of practice and stakeholders.
Disconnected → Mindfulness and Wholeness	Promotes Professionalism, Mindfulness, and Wholeness—Serves as a role model for high ethics and morals; instills pride; gains respect and trust with proactive communication and collaboration. Is constantly developing themselves. Creates a safe and amiable culture designed to encourage creativity and new ideas. Manages risks with experimentation, alternative perspectives, test and evaluation, and prototyping. Recognizes individual and team contributions, innovations, and progress. Encourages acknowledgment of success and setbacks to continuously improve, learn, and innovate. Builds and sustains trust through example, integrity, accountability, and transparency with individuals, across organizational boundaries, and with stakeholders. Bounces back from adversity through optimism and improving personal health, wellness, and stress management.

When internal needs and external conditions converge, they create the demand for change and adaptation. Cultivating adaptive leadership and systems thinking competencies will lead to a sustainable impact on the health system. While health administrators must deal with unplanned challenges, changing technology, shifting realities, sociopolitical challenges, and innovations, adaptive leadership and systems thinking help counter these challenges. By using systems thinking across functional boundaries, health administrators create meaningful conversations to create systemness throughout the system. Systemness includes internal integrity, the goodness of fit, seamlessness, open boundaries, team-based, to service driven, measures of value, coordinated effort, and sustainable change—a systems thinking mind-set. Over time, the commitment of systems thinking applications grows.[26,28,29]

▶ Conclusion

The legacy of current health administrators is to develop future generations of health administrators who facilitate co-creation and adaptive organizations in the health ecosystem. The traditional command and control, production, or linear approach to decision-making are not appropriate for today's health ecosystem challenges. For health administrators, health ecosystem adaptation must become the guiding mechanisms ranging from daily practice to strategic management. For example, strategic management is inclusive of learning or feedback loops and allows the organization to keep pace with rapid rates of change. This approach permits health organizations to function in a more interdependent manner, respond to the changing needs of the community, or leverage each other's resources for better effect. Health administrators, therefore, must become students of change, systems thinkers, and strategic planners. At the heart of strategic management are systems thinking competencies to determine the overall strategies and facilitation of system changes for the organization.[28,29]

▶ Interviews

Interview 2-1: Health Executive Interview

Interview: Participant 1

David E. Womack, MHA, FACHE

Senior Vice President (SVP), Kaiser Permanente

Bakersfield, CA

Interviewed by Douglas Anderson

Summarize your definition of systems thinking. Systems thinking is seeing the forest and the trees. I do my best to ask, "What's the whole picture of an issue?"

Mr. Womack: Systems thinking is understanding the individual components and how those components affect the desired outcome.

How are systems thinking as a competency beneficial to the practice healthcare administration? Leaders and managers?

Mr. Womack: I think systems thinking can be applied by front-line leaders all the way up to national levels. The ability to tease out factors and assess how factors might be changed is critical to influencing outcomes. When you are leading teams at the tactical level, systems thinking is about helping individuals understand the whole, goals, their responsibilities and how they fit or impact the current system, and how the system's parts and changes are related to the desired outcomes. The idea of wholeness, understanding how parts work or don't work together, and the relationships to outcomes can apply at all levels such as at the hospital, community, or national levels.

In what ways can systems thinking be integrated into strategic planning? Other processes such as HRM, revenue cycle, and quality improvement?

Mr. Womack: If you do not have a fair amount of systems thinking in your strategic planning process, you are not doing strategic planning. Strategic planning is about systems thinking or planning for the desired future and taking the steps for getting there tomorrow. Our supply chain is an example of teasing apart the system and integrating systems thinking into improving these processes to affect the overall system. In sum, you are always asking, "What are we trying to influence and what factors contribute the most to produce the desired effect?"

How have you adopted systems thinking in your organization?

Mr. Womack: Community? I am blessed to have organizational development consultant. While I did use the term "systems thinking," I have been challenged to help teams think about the bigger picture, see connections within their processes, and reflect on goals first before diving into details and going down a rabbit trail without thinking about the whole. I have stressed that while team members have energy and passion about their processes, they must understand that they are a piece of the big picture, they must learn how the pieces work together, and they must focus on the system first. A recent example is how our leadership training program emerged in a well-meaning "ad hoc" fashion over the years. We developed an executive leadership education program for high-level executives and then developed a program for lower-level managers. Another senior leader approached the program with a systems approach on how to grow and develop future leaders with familiar themes, competencies, and topics now referred to as the Kaiser Permanente Leadership University. It is now a formal part of the strategic HRM and leader development program.

Why do you believe systems thinking has not readily been adopted by health care or healthcare administrators?

Mr. Womack: The question presupposes systems thinking has not been adopted. Systems thinking is something people talk about but do not necessarily use the formal term. Systems thinking is a reflection of the maturity levels of the individuals in the room. Barriers to adopting systems thinking include the pressure of time and the willingness to invest the time to think through individual parts and pieces. To overcome these barriers, we need to expose individuals to broader initiatives outside their comfort zone and day-to-day jobs.

How can we create a systems thinking culture in health care and prepare future leaders?

Mr. Womack: Leadership and organizational development need to infuse systems thinking but don't use the term. We should start using the term, making others aware of the potential and value, and involving individuals in the thinking and value. Increasing awareness of systems thinking and exposing individuals as part of working complex projects will go a long way. One of my significant challenges has not only been to help individuals, departments, and groups see how their pieces fit within the overall system but identify what is motivating or driving them to change and align their pieces with the bigger picture. This situation takes systems thinking into the human dimension rather than the mechanical dimension. We need to figure out how to make it psychologically safe and create a virtuous or positive spiral cycle of change upstream and sustain the effort.

Interview 2-2: Health Executive and Administrative Fellow Interview

Interview: Participants 2 and 3

James F. Geiger

President, LVH-Muhlenberg

Bethlehem, PA

Madeline Kemp

Administrative Fellow, Lehigh Valley Health Network

Allentown, PA

Summarize your definition of systems thinking.

Mr. Geiger: My definition of systems thinking is to identify relevant variables associated with the intended or unintended consequences of moving forward on good ideas or business plans. *Systems thinking is a lot more than setting up an exam room, making an appointment, seeing patients, and giving them a prescription. Systems thinking should be second nature on how to look at the whole systems and improve the entire process.*

Ms. Kemp: I tend to differentiate systems from strategic planning. While systems thinking may be viewed from the strategic planning and decision-making lens, systems thinking moves beyond traditional silos to consideration for interrelated and interdependent elements, so the system can function better. Systems thinking should involve considering the tangible and intangible benefits of an investment project or significant initiative. We can look at systems thinking from an operational perspective such as the development of our new yet complex $160,000,000 Medical Campus. It is essential to be able to make changes in the business model, adapt to situations, and involve the right people who represent vital processes to minimize delays and generate solutions.

How are systems thinking as a competency beneficial to the practice healthcare administration? Leaders and managers?

Mr. Geiger: Our Family Health Pavilion—volume, the mix of patients, revenue sources, and types of services—provides a great example of a significant strategic initiative experience. The dynamic nature of the environment created a threefold increase in self-pay patients; changes in reimbursement policies such as Center for Medicare and Medicaid Services diagnostic testing; the influence of social services; and higher-volume and higher-risk episodes of care such as opiate-related pregnancies increased, and uncertain budget and taxation policies all eroded our revenue estimates. This strategic business plan was elaborate concerning analysis, committing funds, and doing so in the context of the community. The plan, which involves a complex and lengthy coordination process, is typically 24 months. However, our planning horizon is typically a 20-year outlook. This experience drove our thinking about planning future projects and incorporating more people into the complicated process earlier, rather than later.

Ms. Kemp: The lessons from the Family Health Pavilion are currently being applied to the new Medical Campus project. This experience is teaching me to think through the elements and components of the system to build in more planning processes and people earlier, rather than later, and facilitate change and preparation with scenarios and drills associated with the patient mix and other situations. I want to reiterate: The environmental dynamics requires more forward-thinking, use of scenarios to learn and adapt, more inclusiveness of people earlier due to the complexity of the processes, and overall adaptive leadership. In the future, modeling and forecasting of CMS reimbursement schemes and use of planning scenarios will help teams make better decisions.

In what ways can systems thinking be integrated into strategic planning? HRM, revenue cycle, and quality improvement initiatives?

Mr. Geiger: I will use HRM in the context of our Medical Campus (Cancer and Musculoskeletal Care with eight operating rooms) and Family Health Pavilion experience as the example. First, the HRM process must include more than the posting of vacancies. While the patient experience is second to none, we wanted more problem solvers and quick thinkers to help with putting together the "pieces of the implementation puzzle" as a team. This effort included the finding obvious and the not-so-apparent disconnects in the system associated with implementation processes and flows. These examples represent systems thinking at the front-line level of the organization. Clinical, administrative, and ancillary colleagues are working together, knowing their processes, responsibilities, and interest in the overall system. Getting everyone to the table to problem solve from a systems thinking perspective is a way to employ systems thinking and focus on quality improvement.

Do you believe systems thinking has not readily been adopted by health administrators?

Mr. Geiger: First, as in the case of the Veterans Resource Center, we are incorporating a systems approach—social, cultural, and population health components. Unfortunately, it is more difficult to conduct these projects today because of disincentives (such as lack of payment for the adjunct services that may be provided by such an initiative). Another example is our $3 million Advanced Remote ICU Monitoring Unit, where centrally located intensivists monitor 140 critical care units at six facilities. We have saved lives and salary costs associated with centrally located intensivists. As result of the second set of eyes, we have prevented litigation, we have produced better quality care, but there is no revenue associated with providing this service. This situation stifles systems thinking and creativity to be more "holistic." Second, admittedly, in all my undergraduate, graduate, and continuing medical education experience, the topic has never been addressed in my 43 years. I had to learn hard lessons in applying a systems approach to major projects. It is a new paradigm for individuals in my generation.

Ms. Kemp: It is hard to encourage systems thinking because the organization chart reinforces typical approaches to solving problems in isolation. When I worked at the Veterans Affairs Medical Center, I was exposed to interdisciplinary teams called Patient Aligned Care Teams. When it comes to using systems thinking with other groups in the community, unfortunately, the reimbursement structure does not provide healthcare providers who have limited capacity enough incentive to invest seriously. For example, it can be hard to see some major initiatives, such as those aimed at reducing healthcare utilization, translate into quantifiable and tangible benefits, like reduced expenses. Executive leadership would like to test many ideas, as they would likely improve overall care; however, the environment does not permit such investments because health systems already face slim margins.

How can we create a systems thinking culture in health care and prepare future leaders?

Mr. Geiger: Again, the Family Health Pavilion, Medical Campus, and Veterans Resource Center experience helped my team understand the dependencies and interdependencies in achieving goals. It gave the team the opportunity to learn by seeing how we could help and provide a community benefit and thus improve our bottom line. Systems thinking contributed to this. These are also great case studies. I think the use of case studies and more formal application of systems thinking approaches and tools will go a long way to understanding what works and what does not work. Case studies are a great way to learn what works, does not work, and how to be more successful. Also, we must be able to visualize the intangible benefits as part of case studies. Tangible benefits and hard metrics go hand-in-hand with systems and will make it easier to embrace systems thinking more often.

Ms. Kemp: I would like to reiterate and expand on what Jim has stated. To create a culture of health and prepare future leaders, we must embrace the local community needs assessments and provide appropriate incentives to implement complex projects such as those we have discussed. To create a systems thinking culture and prepare future leaders, I think case studies are best for early careerists, as they provide real-life scenarios on how systems thinking can help professionals through complex strategic and operational environments.

References

1. Berwick D. *Transcript: Donald Berwick on Medicare, Medicaid, 'Rationing' and Who Decides.* In: Galewitz P, ed. Washington, DC: Kaiser Health News; 2011.
2. Berwick D, Hackbarth, AD. Eliminating waste in US Health Care. *J Am Med Assoc (JAMA).* 2012;307(14):1513-1516.
3. Kaplan G, Bo-Linn G, Carayon P, Pronovost P, et al. *Bringing a Systems Approach to Health. Discussion Paper.* Washington, DC: Institute of Medicine and National Academy of Engineering; 2013.

4. Buchbinder SB, Shanks NH. *Introduction to Healthcare Management.* 2nd ed. Burlington, MA: Jones & Bartlett Learning; 2012.

5. Schyve PM. *Leadership in Healthcare Organizations: A Guide To Joint Commission Leadership Standards.* San Diego, CA: Governance Institute; 2009.

6. n.a. *Competencies Assessment Tool.* Chicago, IL: Healthcare Leadership Alliance and the American College of Healthcare Executives (ACHE); 2018.

7. Lawler S. *ACHE: Professional Development Task Force Report 2014–2015 ANNUAL REPORT.* Chicago, IL: American College of Healthcare Executive (ACHE); 2014.

8. n.a. American College of Healthcare Executives (ACHE) Leadership Competency Model. 2015. https://www.ache.org/.

9. Lewis JB, Mccgraatj Robert J, Seidel Lee F. *Essentials of Applied Quantitative Methods for Health Services Managers.* Sudbury, MA: Jones & Bartlett Learning; 2011.

10. Shi L, Singh DA. *Delivering Healthcare in America: A Systems Approach.* 6th ed. Burlington, MA: Jones & Bartlett Learning; 2015.

11. Shi L, Johnson JA. *Public Health Administration: Principles for Population-based Management.* Burlington, MA: Jones & Bartlett Learning; 2014.

12. Stroh D. *Systems Thinking for Social Change: A Practical Guide to Solving Complex Problems, Avoiding Unintended Consequences, and Achieving Lasting Results.* White River Junction, VT: Chelsea Green Publishing; 2015.

13. Lightner DE. *Advanced Performance Improvement in Health Care.* Sudbury, MA: Jones & Bartlett Learning; 2011.

14. Johnson J, Rossow C. *Health Organizations: Theory, Behavior, and Development.* Burlington, MA: Jones & Bartlett Learning; 2018.

15. Bennett AR. Accountable care organizations: principles and implications for hospital administrators. *J Healthcare Manage.* 2012;57(4):244-254.

16. Nobel DJ, Casalino NP. Can accountable care organizations improve population health? should they try? *J Am Med Assoc.* 2013;11:1119-1120.

17. Kapp JM, Simones EJ, DeBiasi A, Kravet SJ. A conceptual framework for a systems thinking approach to US population health. *Systems Res Behav Sci Syst Res.* 2017;34:686-698.

18. Belasen AT, Eisenberg B, Huppertz JW. *Mastering Leadership: A Vital Resource for Healthcare Organizations.* Burlington, MA: Jones & Bartlett Learning; 2015.

19. Rubino L, Esparza S, Chassiakos Y. *New Leadership for Today's Healthcare Professionals: Concepts and Cases.* Burlington, MA: Jones & Bartlett Learning; 2014.

20. n.a. Basic principles of systems thinking as applied to management and leadership. 2016. http://www.systemicleadershipinstitute.org/systemic-leadership/theories/basic-principles -of-systems-thinking-as-applied-to-management-and-leadership-2/.

21. Maccoby M, Norman CL, Norman CJ, Margolies R. *Transforming Healthcare Leadership: A Systems Guide to Improve Patient Care, Decrease Costs, and Improve Population Health.* Hoboken, NJ: Jossey-Bass; 2013.

22. Langabeer JR, Helon J. *Healthcare Operations Management: A Systems Perspective.* 2nd ed. Burlington, MA: Jones & Bartlett Learning; 2016.

23. Griffith JR. Understanding high reliability: are Baldrige recipient models? *J Healthcare Manage.* 2015;60(1):44-61.

24. Porter-O'Grady T, Malloch K. *Quantum Leadership: Advancing Innovation, Transforming Healthcare.* 3rd ed. Burlington, MA: Jones & Bartlett Learning; 2011.

25. APHA. *American Public Health Association (APHA) Leadership Competency Model;* 2015. https://www.apha.org/.

26. Rowitz L. *Public Health Leadership: Putting Principles into Practice.* 3rd ed. Burlington, MA: Jones & Bartlett Learning; 2014.

27. Rowitz L. *Public Health of the 21st Century: The Prepared Leader.* Burlington, MA: Jones & Bartlett Learning; 2006.

28. AUPHA. *Association of University Programs in Health Administration (AUPHA)/Body of Knowledge (BOK) for Health Management and Policy.* Arlington, VA: Association of University Programs in Health Administration (AUPHA); 2012.

29. Lightner DE. *The Basics of Health Care Performance Improvement: A Lean Six Sigma Approach.* Burlington, MA: Jones & Bartlett Learning; 2013.

30. AONE. *American Organization of Nurse Executives (AONE) Leadership Competency Models.* American Organization of Nurse Executives (AONE); 2015.

31. Linder N, Frakes J. A New Path to Understanding Systems Thinking. *Systems Thinker*; 2018.

32. Lachney K. How to Avoid the Top 5 Medical Billing Errors. *Health System Management*: ADVANCE Healthcare Network, an Elite CE company; 2016.

33. n.a. Survey: Hospital CFOs say multiple projects force Revenue Cycle to Backburner. *Becker's Hospital CFO Report: Becker's Hospital Review*; 2013.

34. n.a. 4 Best practices for Revenue Cycle Management system replacement. 2013. Financial Management. Available at: https://www.beckershospitalreview.com/finance/4-best-practices-for-revenue-cycle-management-system-replacement.html.

35. Dunn A. Empowered patient missing in Revenue Cycle Management: Part 1; 2017.

36. Lachney K. Medical billing denials are avoidable: how to help prevent the top 5. *Viewpoints: Change Healthcare*; 2016.

37. Heifetz R, Grashow A. *The Practice of Adaptive Leadership: Tools and Tactics for Changing Your Organization and the World.* Cambridge, MA: Harvard Business Press; 2009.

38. Senge PM. *The Fifth Discipline: The Art and Practice of the Learning Organization.* New York City Doubleday/Currency; 2006.

39. Richmond B. Systems thinking/system dynamics: let's just get on with it. *SystDyn Rev.* 1994;10(2-3):135-157.

40. Meadows DH. *Thinking in Systems, A Primer.* White River Junction, VT: Chelsea Green Publishing Company; 2008.

41. Sethi R. Virginia Mason study shows team method prevents overuse of spinal fusion surgery. 2017. https://www.virginiamason.org/virginia-mason-study-shows-team-method-prevents-overuse-of-spinal-fusion-surgery.

42. Group GSW. The "Top 5" lists in primary care: meeting the responsibility of professionalism. *Arch Intern Med.* 2011;171(15):1385-1390.

43. Blackmore CC, Mecklenburg RS, Kaplan GS. At Virginia Mason, collaboration among providers, employers, and health plans to transform care cut costs and improved quality. *Health Affairs (Millwood).* 2011;30(9):1680-1687.

44. Hoffman A, Emanuel EJ. Reengineering us health care. *JAMA.* 2013;309(7):661-662.

45. IOM. *Best Care at Lower Cost: The Path to Continuously Learning Health Care in America.* Washington, DC: National Academy of Sciences, Institute of Medicine (IOM); 2012.

46. Johnson JH, Haskell HW, Baraxh PR. *Case Studies and Patient Safety: Foundations for Core Competencies.* Burlington, MA: Jones & Bartlett Learning; 2016.

47. Doty E. The Upward Spiral: Bootstrapping Systemic Change. *Systems Thinking.* Leverage Networks, Inc., Pegasus Communications; 2016.

48. Haigh M. Why leaders need to be systems thinkers. *Business Perspectives.* Open University; 2016.

49. Haines SG. *The Manager's Pocket Guide to Systems Thinking and Learning.* Amherst, MA: HRD Press; 1998.

50. Haines SG. *The Systems Thinking Approach to Strategic Planning and Management.* Boca Raton, FL: CRC Press; 2000.

51. Chassin MR, Loeb JM. High-reliability health care: getting there from here. *Milbank Q.* 2013;91(3): 459-490.

52. AHRQ. Patient safety primer: high reliability. PSNet; 2016. Retrieved from https://psnet.ahrq.gov/primers/primer/31

CHAPTER 3

Systems Thinking for Clinician Education, Leadership, and Practice

▶ ## Why It Is Important in Clinical Practice

The Need for Systems Thinking: Medical Errors

Nearly two decades have passed since the Institute of Medicine (IOM) released the alarming report *To Err Is Human: Building a Safer Heath System*, conveying between 44,000 and 98,000 deaths in hospitals each year due to preventable medical errors.[1] A medical error is defined as "failure of a planned action to be completed as intended or the use of a wrong plan to achieve an aim."[1] During the provision of care, medical errors such as adverse drug events, blood transfusion errors, surgical injuries and wrong side/site surgeries, improper use of restraints with resulting injury or death, falls, burns, pressure ulcers, and mistaken patient identities may happen.[1] High-risk areas were the emergency departments, operating rooms (ORs), and intensive care units (ICUs).[1] In addition to the loss of human life, the estimated annual expense of care and potentially lost income were between $17 and $29 billion in U.S. hospitals.[1] A comprehensive strategy was recommended in which the providers of care, the government, business, and industry along with consumers could reduce or prevent errors.[1] The report concluded that errors do not occur from individual recklessness, but faulty systems, processes, and mistakes could be prevented by redesigning the healthcare delivery system at all levels to enhance safety.[1] The IOM suggested an intensive four-tier approach presented in **BOX 3.1**. A 50% reduction in medical errors in 5 years was proposed by generating a national focus with mandatory reporting.[1]

In 2001, the IOM released a second report titled *Crossing the Quality Chasm: A New Health System for the 21st Century*, which suggested that an enormous chasm still existed between the health care provided and that which Americans could have. Based on the biomedical model, health care has been devoted to acute episodic care with little focus on preventive medicine or population health. Medical technology was and continues to grow at an astronomical rate adding to the complexity of care

---

BOX 3.1 Four-Tier Approach for Medical Error Reduction[1]

1. Establishing a national focus to create leadership, research, tools, and protocols to enhance knowledge base and safety.
2. Identifying and learning from errors by developing a nationwide, public, mandatory reporting system and encouraging healthcare organizations and practitioners to develop and participate in voluntary reporting systems.
3. Raising performance standards and expectations for improvements in safety through the actions of oversight organizations, professional groups, and group purchasers of health care.
4. Implementing safety systems in healthcare organizations to ensure safe practices at the delivery level.

Reproduced from Institute of Medicine. 2000. To Err Is Human: Building a Safer Health System. Washington, DC: The National Academies Press. https://doi.org/10.17226/9728.

BOX 3.2 Six Core Aims to Reinvent the Healthcare System[2]

Safe: Avoiding injuries to patients from the care that is intended to help them.
Effective: Providing services based on scientific knowledge to all who could benefit and refraining from providing services to those who would not likely benefit.
Patient Centered: Providing care that is respectful of and responsive to individual patient preferences, needs, and values and ensuring that patient values guide all clinical decisions.
Timely: Reducing waits and sometimes harmful delays for both those who receive and those who give care.
Efficient: Avoiding waste, including waste of equipment, supplies, ideas, and energy.
Equitable: Providing care that does not vary in quality because of personal characteristics such as gender, ethnicity, geographic location, and socioeconomic status.

Reproduced from Institute of Medicine. 2001. Crossing the Quality Chasm: A New Health System for the 21st Century. Washington, DC: The National Academies Press. https://doi.org/10.17226/10027.

---

and fostering specialists to safely manage diagnostic tests and restorative treatments to individuals with chronic conditions.[2] The provision of care is highly complex, requiring communication, collaboration, and safe handoffs between providers who can at times slow down care rather than enhance safe and effective care.[2] Traditionally, healthcare providers (hospitals, physicians, and other health organizations) have operated in silos without obtaining complete information about the patient's condition to successfully manage care, leading to medical errors and unsafe care. The healthcare systems were (and still are) decentralized, fragmented, and poorly organized. As described in **BOX 3.2**, the report suggested six core aims, a strategy to reinvent the healthcare system.[2] If health care could achieve these aims, the patient care experience would be safer, more satisfying, and integrated.

The report also provided a blueprint for the 21st century or 10 rules to redesign the healthcare delivery systems as listed in **BOX 3.3**. Major themes include holistic care, collaboration, safety, transparency, and evidence based.[2]

BOX 3.3 The 10 Rules to Redesign Health Care[2]

1. Care is based on continuous healing relationships.
2. Care is customized according to the patient's needs and values.
3. The patient is the source of control.
4. Knowledge is shared and information flows freely.
5. Decision-making is evidence based.
6. Safety is a system property.
7. Transparency is necessary.
8. Needs are anticipated.
9. Waste is continuously decreased.
10. Cooperation among clinicians is a priority.

Reproduced from Institute of Medicine. 2001. Crossing the Quality Chasm: A New Health System for the 21st Century. Washington, DC: The National Academies Press. https://doi.org/10.17226/10027.

The IOM Committee requested that the Agency for Health Research and Quality identify 15 high-volume chronic/common conditions and develop core processes to improve outcomes.[2] The committee suggested applying scientific knowledge and evidence to clinical practice and using information technology to transform the healthcare system.[2]

The National Patient Safety Goals

In 2002, The Joint Commission established the National Patient Safety Goals (NPSGs) program. Developed in consultation with a panel of healthcare providers (physicians, pharmacists, nurses, risk managers, and others involved in the patient care process), they identified emerging high-risk safety issues, advising The Joint Commission of potential steps for correction.[3] After solicitation from key stakeholders, The Joint Commission determined the highest safety priority and provided the first set of NPSGs that were effective January 1, 2003.[3]

According to the Veterans Administration National Center for Patient Safety, the 2003 Joint Commission on Accreditation of Healthcare Organization Patient Safety Goals were:

- Improve the accuracy of patient identification.
- Improve the effectiveness of communication among caregivers.
- Improve the safety of using high-alert medications.
- Eliminate wrong-site, wrong-patient, and wrong-procedure surgery.
- Improve the safety of using infusion pumps.
- Improve the effectiveness of clinical alarm systems.[4]

Since implementation, The Joint Commission has provided ongoing education with Sentinel Event Alerts, standards and survey processes, performance measures, and educational materials.[3] Goals change yearly based on the assessed needs. Although significant progress has been made in many of the goals, wrong-site, wrong-patient, and wrong-procedure surgery—being the sentinel event that is most frequently reported to The Joint Commission—continues to plague the healthcare system, with 1,196 such events reported through September 30, 2015.[5]

The 100,000 Lives Campaign

In December 2004, the Institute for Healthcare Improvement (IHI) launched the 100,000 lives campaign to improve safety and effectiveness in health care.[6] This aggressive 18-month program was designed from best practice protocols of medical specialties and related government organizations to successfully decrease mortality and morbidity in the United States.[6] The nation's hospitals (5,759 in 2004) were invited to participate in the program, demonstrating their commitment to patient safety, decreasing mortality, morbidity, and transparency (reporting results to their community).[6]

Six peer-reviewed interventions were selected:

- Deploy rapid response teams.
- Deliver reliable, evidence-based care for acute myocardial infarction.
- Prevent adverse drug events.
- Prevent central catheter infections.
- Prevent surgical site infection.
- Prevent ventilator-associated pneumonia.[7]

Endorsed by a plethora of federal, national, state organizations, hospital, medical, nursing societies, and quality improvement organizations, a powerful national infrastructure was created to foster change and continued collaboration to transform health care.[6] At the end of the campaign, approximately 3,100 hospitals in the United States participated with more than 122,000 lives saved.[8]

The 5 Million Lives Campaign

Building on the momentum of the 100,000 Lives Campaign, the IHI launched the 5 Million Lives Campaign aimed at enhancing the improvement of medical care in the United States by significantly reducing levels of morbidity and mortality.[9] Over a 2-year period, December 12, 2006 through December 9, 2008, IHI and its partners encouraged hospitals and other healthcare providers to work in six key areas as described in **BOX 3.4** to reduce harm and death, in addition to the six interventions first introduced in the 100,000 Lives Campaign. Although the total impact of lives saved is unknown, the campaign made impressive strides to improve the quality and safety of health care with over 4,050 hospitals participating.[9]

The IHI Triple Aim

In response to increasing healthcare costs, quality concerns, chronic health conditions, and an aging population, the IHI developed the Triple Aim, a framework for healthcare improvement, and an approach for optimizing health system performance. The framework consists of simultaneously pursuing three dimensions (thus, the Triple Aim): improving the patient experience of care, the health of the population, and reducing the per capita cost of health care.[10] Based on six phases of pilot testing in over 100 organizations worldwide, the IHI recommended a change process to include: identification of target populations; definition of systems aims and measures; development of a portfolio of work that is strong to move system-level results and rapid testing to adapt to local needs.[10] Initially, an IHI team developed a

BOX 3.4 The 5 Million Lives Campaign Peer-Reviewed Interventions[9]

1. Prevent pressure ulcers by reliably using science-based guidelines for preventing serious and common complications.
2. Reduce Methicillin-Resistant *Staphylococcus aureus* infection (MRSA) by making basic changes in infection control processes throughout the hospital.
3. Prevent harm from high-alert medications starting with a focus on anticoagulants, sedatives, narcotics, and insulin.
4. Reduce surgical complications by reliably implementing changes in care recommended by the Surgical Care Improvement Project.
5. Deliver reliable, evidence-based care for congestive heart failure to reduce hospital readmission.
6. Get Boards on board by defining and spreading new and leveraged processes for the hospitals' Board of Directors, so that they can effectively accelerate the improvement of care.

Reproduced with permission from The Institute for Healthcare Improvement in Boston, Massachusetts (www.ihi.org). Accessed at: http://www.ihi.org/Engage/Initiatives/Completed/5MillionLivesCampaign/Pages/default.aspx.

FIGURE 3.1 Timeline of Reports, Quality, and Safety Initiatives

concept design and described a set of five design components of a system that would help fulfill the IHI Triple Aim, including:

- Focus on individuals and families.
- Redesign of the primary care services and structure.
- Population health management.
- Cost control platform.
- System integration and execution.[10]

The IHI Triple Aim was implemented in 2007 and is presently ongoing. The Patient Protection and Affordable Care Act signed in 2010 calls for continued healthcare improvements comprising access, quality, and cost of care. As shown in **FIGURE 3.1** from the timeline of reports, quality and safety initiatives dating from 1999, countless healthcare organizations and providers have worked tirelessly to decrease medical errors and provide safe evidence-based care.

Still, our healthcare system, which intends to heal patients, is plagued by the opposite effect, leading to unintended and unnecessary deaths in alarming rates. In 2013, estimates up to 440,000 Americans are dying annually from preventable hospital errors.[11] Approximately 1,000 people die from preventable errors daily, making medical errors the third leading cause of death in the United States.[12] This underscores the need for patients to protect themselves and their families from harm, and for hospitals to make patient safety a priority.[11] Based on this evidence, a movement from personal effort and individual care to systems-based care is desperately needed to accelerate the improvement of healthcare quality and safety.[13]

▶ How Can Systems Thinking Be Applied?

Systems Thinking and the Healthcare Disciplines

Systems thinking is the cornerstone of systems-based practice (SBP) and a core competency across all healthcare disciplines.[14] Several disciplines have embraced the systems thinking concept, especially nursing and general/family practice. If it is not introduced as part of their undergraduate or graduate training, it is highly unlikely that systems thinking will be introduced to them within their career due to other educational demands.[15] When students are exposed to systems thinking in their formal training, it sends a message regarding what is important and sets the tone for what is valued and expected in their professional life.[15]

Nursing

As you recall from previous chapters, systems thinking means viewing the organization based on the needs of patients, providers, and employees and comprised of interdependent people, equipment, products, and processes, all working toward a common purpose. Systems thinking allows the registered nurse (RN) to see beyond the bedside and be able to change processes, effectively impacting patient safety by preventing errors, ultimately providing a positive patient experience and outcome. Systems thinking allows the RN to see patterns, connections and interactions, and their impact with regard to patient care.[16] The RN can understand how the direct care of their patient is linked to the department and ultimately healthcare systems outcomes.[17] So, how do we educate and train nurses to systems think?

Nursing Education

The Quality and Safety Education for Nurses (QSEN) initiative was developed in 2005 with an overall goal to prepare future nurses with the knowledge, skills, and attitudes to continuously improve the quality and safety of the healthcare systems in which they work by integrating quality and safety competencies into nursing education.[18] Funded by the Robert Wood Johnson Foundation, three phases from 2005 to 2012 shaped six core competencies, faculty expertise, competencies in textbooks, licensing, accreditation, and certification standards impacting nursing education from the pre-nursing licensure to the doctoral level.[19] Building on the 2001 IOM report, the six core competencies include patient-centered care, teamwork and collaboration, evidence-based practice, quality improvement, safety, and informatics that are defined in **TABLE 3.1**.[18]

Mastery at an individual level allows nurses to comprehend the significance of their actions at a systems level, ultimately understanding how "one nurse's action can influence the success of an organization's quality and safety outcomes."[20] Dolansky and Moore (2013) suggest systems thinking is on a continuum, where it is expressed by nursing care as an increasing ability to move from a reliance on authority to interprofessional collaboration. This process can be applied to teams and organizations as a whole to impact cause and effect; complex problems are then solved through collaborative efforts of individuals contributing their knowledge, skills, and abilities to improve the greater whole (**TABLE 3.2**).[13]

TABLE 3.1 Quality and Safety Education for Nurses' Competencies[18]

Competency	Definition
Patient-Centered Care	Recognize the patient or designee as the source of control and full partner in providing compassionate and coordinated care based on respect for the patient's preferences, values, and needs.
Teamwork and Collaboration	Function effectively within nursing and interprofessional teams, fostering open communication, mutual respect, and shared decision-making to achieve quality patient care.
Evidence-Based Practice	Integrate best current evidence with clinical expertise and patient/family preferences and values for the delivery of optimal health care.
Quality Improvement	Use data to monitor the outcomes of care processes and use improvement methods to design and test changes to continuously improve the quality and safety of healthcare systems.
Safety	Minimize risk of harm to patients and providers through both system effectiveness and individual performance.
Informatics	Use information and technology to communicate, manage knowledge, mitigate error, and support decision-making.

Modified from QSEN. Competencies.qsen.org. http://qsen.org/competencies.

A number of nurse educators reported that the QSEN competencies are already incorporated into their curriculum, but they suggested that in the practice setting, this integration has only been at the individual level of care, rather than a systems level.[13] An interview with nursing faculty Professor Keith and Dr. Dobrzykowski substantiated the implementation of QSEN as well as systems thinking in both undergraduate and graduate nursing curricula.

RN to BSN Programs

There are a vast number of RNs with Associate Degrees in Nursing returning to college for their Bachelor of Science in Nursing (BSN) degrees. In 2016, approximately 47% of BSN graduates completed the RN to BSN program.[21] Unique to this group of students is their healthcare experience, which may serve as a foundation for building leaders in quality, safety, and systems thinking in healthcare organizations. Incorporating systems thinking in the RN to BSN curriculum may well

TABLE 3.2 Examples of Continuums of Systems Thinking for QSEN Domains[13]

QSEN Competency	Personal Effort/Individual Care			Systems Thinking/Systems Care
Patient-Centered Care	Document the presence and extent of patients' pain.	Use common definitions, terms, and rating scales in documenting my patients' pain.	Formulate pain management plan with my patients, their families, and other healthcare professionals.	Participate in medical record review of our unit's pain documentation.
Evidence-Based Practice	Differentiate clinical opinion from research and evidence summaries.	Discuss conflicting evidence in the literature with my colleagues.	Question the rationale for routine care approaches in my unit that are not evidence based.	Participate in writing unit-level standards of practice that are evidence based.
Teamwork and Collaboration	Ensure that my patients are ready for discharge by making sure they have their prescriptions.	Formulate discharge plan with my patients, their families, and other healthcare professionals.	Solicit input from other team members to improve my team performance.	Participate in improving the discharge process through team meetings to structure communication during the patients' hospital stay.
Safety	Wash my hands at appropriate times while caring for my patients.	Get patients and families to participate in the campaign to reduce infection by hand washing.	Observe other nurses' hand washing technique and provide feedback.	Study the workarounds in my unit and create a cause and effect diagram to summarize why nurses do not wash their hands.

Quality Improvement	Ensure that I care for central catheters using evidence-based practice.	Have a peer observe my central catheter dressing change, so that I can improve my performance.	Review the data for central catheter infection rates in our units.	Participate in a quality improvement project to improve compliance with central catheter bundle in our unit.
Informatics	Protect the confidentiality of my patients' health information in electronic health records.	Attend in-service training updates to learn about new laws regarding health information protection.	Help design patient information flyers describing the patients' and families' rights to information confidentiality in electronic health records.	Participate in an agency-wide committee to update the agency regarding electronic health records system.

Dolanski MA, Moore SM. Quality and safety education for nurses (QSEN): the key is systems thinking. *Online J Issues Nurs*. 2013; 18(3):1-12.

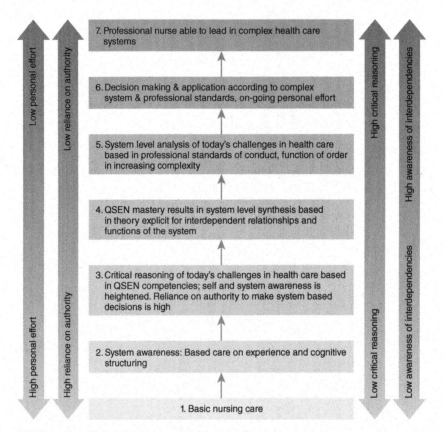

FIGURE 3.2 Systems Level Awareness Model

Reproduced from Phillips JM, Stalter AM, Dolansky MA, Lopez GM. Fostering future leadership in quality and safety in health care through systems thinking. J Profess Nurs. 2016;32(1):15–24.

provide the framework for these up-and-coming nurse leaders to improve quality and safety in their clinical practice environment.[17] **FIGURE 3.2** displays the seven progressive phases of learning, providing a means for students to think and act at a systems level.[17]

In the model, action is displayed in the double-headed vertical arrows lateral to the steps with SBP behaviors of personal effort, reliance on authority, critical reasoning, and awareness of interdependencies.[17] Personal effort and reliance on authority are characterized inversely to critical reasoning and awareness of interdependencies.[17] As the RN advances in education, through the steps, low personal effort, low reliance on authority are replaced with high critical reasoning and high awareness of interdependencies. The process of increasing the RNs systems awareness is summarized in **TABLE 3.3**.

This can be accomplished if nurses are allowed to be fully engaged in the healthcare system, practicing to the full extent of their education and training, and become full partners with physicians and other healthcare professionals in redesigning health care in the United States.[22] Interviews with Professor Keith, Dr. Dobrzykowski, and Ms. DeShore stressed the importance of interprofessional collaborative practice to enhance the safe delivery of care.

TABLE 3.3 Phases of Systems Level Awareness

Phase	Description—Systems Level Awareness
Phase I Basic Nursing Care	RNs with an Associate Degree in Nursing or a diploma seek to obtain their BSN. They have a basic understanding of nursing care. The RNs, because of their prior education and work experience, have preexisting knowledge of the healthcare system.
Phase II Systems Awareness	RNs, because of their preexisting experience, have the cognitive structure or basic mental processes to make sense of their role and the healthcare environment in which they have worked.
Phase III Critical Reasoning	The RNs have the ability to conceptualize, analyze, question, and evaluate challenges faced in health care based on the QSEN competencies. The RNs' perception of self and self-awareness is heightened, suggesting that a systems-based curriculum focused on the BSN Essentials can be instrumental in heightening systems awareness and permit the RN to critically analyze clinical situations. This self-awareness is vital to enhancing systems awareness.
Phase IV QSEN Mastery	QSEN mastery provides a basis for understanding the impact of nursing on patient care and teams, factual information and evidence, and the overall impact of nursing on quality and safety for the entire health organization.
Phase V Systems Level Analysis	The RN starts to analyze the system based on recognized standards of care, understanding the complexity of the healthcare system.
Phase VI Decision-Making	The RNs embrace professional standards and strive to ensure safe patient-centered care decisions while recognizing and respecting the contributions by all members of the healthcare team. Ultimately achieving positive patient outcomes minimizes the negative impact to the healthcare organization.
Phase VII Leading	RNs, as professionals, understand the increasing complexity of the healthcare system, its functionality, and their role within the system. The professional nurses will personally strive for quality and safety in patient care. Using a systems thinking approach, they will have a comprehensive understanding of the interdependencies and ability to lead in the complex healthcare systems.

Adapted from Phillips JM, Staltler AM, Dolansky MA, and McKee Lopez G. Fostering future leadership in quality and safety through systems thinking. *J Profess Nurs*. 2016 32 (1):15–24.

Nurse Leaders and Professional Development Practitioners

To support systems thinking awareness for direct care nurses, Statler and Mota cite six competencies of QSEN, with a seventh systems thinking competency, highlighting evidence-based practice recommendations for use by both the nurse leader and professional development practitioners.[20] Nursing leadership plays a critical role in systems thinking. Ensuring the availability of human resources (staffing) and collaborative tools, promoting shared goals of quality and efficiency, designing a process that improves quality, and providing technology and a shared governance structure are all examples of ways nurses leaders can support the direct care nurse. Chief nursing officers are in an excellent position to champion a systems thinking approach to improve quality and safety.[23] Most chief nursing officers work across several departments and patient care areas, where they may provide support, advice, critical thinking, and analytical skills to improve patient care.[23,24] This requires not only a focus on the clinical aspect of patient care but also on all of the support systems that enable care.[25] Systems components include the patient, staff, equipment, and the environment in which care is provided.[25] Many organizations have recognized their contributions, having them partner with other chief executives and physician leaders to achieve an exceptional patient experience and high-quality outcomes.[23,26]

Ongoing systems thinking education is imperative. Professional development practitioners can incorporate a systems thinking approach into patient-centered competencies, safety and quality indicators, and interprofessional collaborative practice into nursing education.[20] These steps will help foster a culture of transparency, quality, and safety with a focus on error prevention and improved patient outcomes.[20]

Nursing Measurement of Systems Thinking

Moore, Dolansky, Singh, Palmieri, and Alemi developed a reliable tool for measuring systems thinking in quality improvement work. Identifying the conceptual domains of systems thinking, 30 instrument items were initially tested for content validity.[16] After revisions, 26 items were presented for psychometric testing in over 550 healthcare professionals and health professions students.[16] Finally, 20 items were assessed for reliability with pre–post testing, and internal consistency teaching used a Cronbach's alpha with a coefficient of 0.89.[16] This Systems Thinking Scale uses 20-item statements, 5-point Likert-like scale with 0 = never, 1 = seldom, 2 = some of the time, 3 = often, and 4 = most of the time, summing the responses ranging from 0 to 80.[16] The respondents are asked to indicate their agreement with the phrase "*When I want to make an improvement ....*" followed by 20 instrument items, rating them using the Likert-like scale.[16] The Systems Thinking Tool can potentially increase the understanding of one of the mechanisms (systems thinking) by which the continuous quality improvement processes achieve their results, increase knowledge of social capital on continuous quality improvement teams, and improve efforts of future continuous quality improvement teams.[16]

Systems Thinking in Nursing Practice

A research study by Tetuan, Ohm, Kinzie, McMaster, Moffitt, and Mosier examined whether systems thinking improves the perception of safety culture and patient safety.[27] The purpose of the study was to improve patient safety in medication administration through a systems thinking education program (STEP).[27] The aims of the study were to identify nursing workarounds related to medication administration, assess changes in medication events and workarounds after a one-year STEP.[27] Additionally, the study assessed changes in systems thinking and safety culture after STEP and determined whether a correlation existed between safety culture and systems thinking.[27] Pre- and post-comparisons (using medication safety huddles and the monthly STEP) were measured using the Safety Attitude Questionnaire and the Systems Thinking Scale.[27] Direct observation of medication administrations and workarounds in eight nursing units were completed by trained observers pre- and post-STEP.[27] The results revealed a significant decrease (from 9.4% to 4.2%) in medication events post-intervention.[27] Nurses' perception of safety culture was more positive after the STEP than pre intervention ($p = 0.029$) as well as the post-intervention systems thinking scores ($p = 0.013$).[27] Additionally, the Safety Attitude Questionnaire and the Systems Thinking Scale revealed a positive correlation ($r = 0.297$, $p < 0.001$). In this study, the STEP intervention increased systems thinking awareness, enhanced patient safety in medication administration, and contributed to a positive perception of safety culture.[27]

▶ Medical Practice

Integration of Systems and Complexity Theory

In the 1950s, medicine began to understand that illness should not be thought of as a fault of certain parts of the body but as a response or mode of behavior of a living human organism in reaction to forces as it moves in space in time.[28] The cause of illness should be examined as a dynamic interaction of the nature of the individual and the nature of the environment at a specific point in time.[28] From a systems thinking perspective, relieving stress in parts of the outer system can benefit the health or mental health of an individual more effectively than attempting to modify his/her processes directly.[28] For example, modifying dysfunctional family patterns and relationships can often help a troubled child more expeditiously than trying to treat the child individually.[28] Poverty, malnutrition, forms of prejudice, discrimination, and inadequate education/schooling can leave scars on one's personality as deep as those experienced by poor parenting or stress from a broken home.[28] Therefore, in the systems thinking approach, the impact of all stresses depends on the context and the culture in which they are experienced.[28] Culture creates the framework for understanding the patient's perception and/or experience of health.[28]

The founders of family medicine, generalist physicians, had an institutive understanding of systems theory and the biopsychosocial model, based on their daily working experience, be it delivering babies, making home visits, managing chronic illness and end-of-life care.[29] In the 1970s, general/family practice physicians began conversations on systems and complexity science, leading to the recognition that systems and complexity science offered an increased understanding of illness in individual patients, their families, and the community.[30] Family therapists were the first to recognize the impact of variables in understanding observed patterns of health, wellness, and illness.[30] The realization was that patients would be better understood belonging to interconnected, overlapping systems that act, react, and influence in nonlinear ways, with an agent's interaction through multicausal feedback loops.[30] To understand and treat a patient, providers must consider the effects of these overlapping variables such as family, community, and work.[30]

Physicians placed a high degree of confidence in the complexity of systems and complexity science to understand the nature of disease and medical care.[30] General/family practice providers recognized the need to understand chaos theory to guide their delivery of care.[30] The characteristics of systems and complexity terms in the general/family practice domain were defined by the relationship between physician and patient; thinking about the connection between the individual patient and his/her illness; embracing the unique multilevel and nonlinear properties of living systems and as a discipline; and transcending the dualistic separation of mind and body.[30]

At the turn of the 21st century, physicians, academics, and researchers employed systems and complexity science to actual provider issues, professional leadership, and the physician–patient relationship.[30] At this time, complexity and systems science were applied to the organization and function of the healthcare system, emphasizing the influence of attractors on the operations of healthcare system organization and their provision of clinical care.[30] Since 2005, there has been a movement from theory to practice.[30] Thus, the general/family practice provider and the healthcare system must understand their environment from a systems perspective and adapt to the specific needs of the community and the individuals they serve.

Systems-Based Practice

Guralnick, Ludwig, and Englander suggest that the system underlies everything providers do in a medical profession.[31] Systems thinking is the cornerstone of SBP.[32] SBP can be thought of as an analytical tool, another way of looking at the world, both of which can improve the delivery of care and change.[32] At the center is the need to understand the complex healthcare systems and the ability to transverse the complexity for the benefit of the patient and lead or actively participate in a process to improve the system.[32] SBP is the fundamental link in preparing physician leaders for partaking in and improving the system of health care.[31,32] Strong interprofessional and communication skills are essential for interacting with the plethora of patients, families, and interprofessional team members as well as other stakeholders, penetrating the large barriers that exist interprofessionally, as well as recognizing and embracing the diversity of the professional culture.

SBP competencies are being incorporated into undergraduate, graduate medical education, and residency programs.[32] Guralnick, Ludwig, and Englander provide seven domains of competency for SBP. The seven domains of competency are summarized in **TABLE 3.4**.

Although SBP competencies are required in undergraduate, graduate education, and residency programs, some practicing physicians lack the knowledge and skills related to systems thinking and SBP. Many specialty boards are now incorporating SBP into the certification and recertification process.[32]

Residency Training Programs

Graduate and professional education programs set the standard for what is later practiced in real life. The Accreditation Council for Graduate Education and the American Board of Medical Specialists categorized six core competencies essential

TABLE 3.4 Seven Domains of Competency for Systems-Based Practice[31,32]

Competency	Domains of Competency
Competency 1	Can work effectively in various healthcare delivery settings and systems relevant to their clinical specialty.
Competency 2	Can coordinate patient care within the health system relevant to their clinical specialty.
Competency 3	Can incorporate considerations of cost awareness and risk-benefit analysis in patient and/or population-based care as it is appropriate.
Competency 4	Can advocate for quality patient care and optimal patient care systems.
Competency 5	Can work in interprofessional teams to enhance patient safety and improve patient care quality.
Competency 6	Can participate in systems errors and implement potential systems solutions.
Competency 7	Knows how to advocate for the promotion of health and the prevention of disease and injury in populations.

Modified from Guralnick S, Ludwig S, Englander R. Domain of competence: Systems-based practice. *Acad Pediatr*. 2014; 14(2 Suppl): S70-9.

for residents (and physicians) to deliver exceptional medical care: patient care, medical knowledge, practice-based learning and improvement, interpersonal and communication skills, professionalism, and SBP.[32] Falling outside of the realm of conventional medical education, SBP has been difficult to define and incorporate into training and practice.[32] Residents are expected to demonstrate an understanding, an awareness, and responsiveness to the larger system of health care, as well as the ability to request other resources in the system to maximize care.[32]

Systems Thinking in Practice

Residency programs have struggled to include practice-based learning and SBP in an ambulatory setting.[33] Colbert, Myers, Cable, Ogden, Mirkes, McNeal, and Skeen evaluated a very unique program in which residents created and led a practice-improvement council in the resident led clinic. Through the Continuity Clinic Ownership in Resident Education (CCORE) Council, the internal medicine residents led initiatives to expand their knowledge in practice management, quality improvement, and patient satisfaction.[33] Using grounded theory, they examined the residents' perspectives on the CCORE Council. **TABLE 3.5** summarizes the six major themes derived from the four one-hour focus groups involving 12 residents over a nine-month period.[33]

TABLE 3.5 Major Themes from CCORE Focus Groups[33]	
Systems thinking and systems-based care skills.	Residents acknowledged they worked within a microsystem, with a number of different stakeholders and interrelationships which are reliant on interdisciplinary teamwork.
Improving quality of care.	Residents gained an increase understanding of potential barriers to care in the clinic setting including the lack of follow-up.
Improved clinic efficiency.	Residents identified inefficiencies in the clinic patient experience.
Ownership of patients.	Residents focused on enhancing efficiency, effectiveness, and quality of care leading to greater ownership of the clinic patients.
Need for improved communication.	Residents recognized the need for communication to other members of the residency program quality improvement initiatives.
Springboard for research.	Residents recognized the need for data and opportunity for research quality from the CCORE.

The residents were asked what knowledge skills and abilities they learned from this CCORE that they had not previously received in their residency program. The residents cited empowerment, practice development and management skills, the ability to transfer what they learned to other areas of their residency program, enhanced communication, increased understanding of the clinical microsystem in which they worked, and creativity in problem solving.[33] The residents also shared an increase in their experience working in the clinic with empowerment for change, increased morale, a voice (being listened to), practice management improvements, unity, efficacy of group, and an enhanced understanding of their clinical environment.[33] Thus, the overall experience was positive, allowing the residents the ability to initiate a SBP and practice-based learning improvements.

Gillen, Ramirez, Farineau, Hoke, Schimer, Williams, and Lau describe an innovative project using interdisciplinary work groups to educate surgical residents in SBP.[34] After acquiring leadership support, interdisciplinary work groups were formed with residents, nursing (from the ICUs, ORs, pre- and postoperative areas, and medical/surgical floors), scrub techs, pharmacists, nurse practitioners and physician assistants, occupational and physical therapists, case managers, electronic health record programmers, social workers, nursing assistants, and unit clerks.[34] A total of 140 participants were organized into 13 interdisciplinary work groups aimed at identifying and developing solutions to systems issues that plagued healthcare providers on a daily basis.[34] At the first meeting, the work groups identified a comprehensive list of commonly encountered systems issues. A total of

13 systems-based issues were selected.[34] At the second meeting, the team members examined the issues, including how the issues affected all team members.[34] After further defining the problems, they described the current state and an ideal state. Potential solutions were generated. At their last meeting, each work group developed their chosen solution into a formal proposal, including an implementation plan.[34] Paging etiquette standards in the OR, medication documentation in the OR, and surgical and trauma ICU patients admitted to medical ICU paging guidelines were three of the systems-based issues that were solved by the work groups. Pre- and post-surveys of participants using the Teamwork Attitude Questionnaire demonstrated a significant improvement in teamwork and communication.[34] These work groups provide an excellent example of how systems thinking and interdisciplinary collaboration can be used to solve complex systems issues.

Physician Leadership

Physicians must realize that significant systems changes need to occur in health care to improve quality and safety. Effective physician leadership is critical to address the fundamental issues related to the Triple Aim.[23] Active leadership by physicians as service line directors, engaged members of the C-suite, and the Board of Directors fosters a collaborative environment that values not only the business aspect of care (reducing costs) but also aligns physicians to enhance the patient experience (quality and satisfaction) and ultimately improve the population health.[23] It is imperative that we welcome and help develop our physician leaders by providing them with essential knowledge, skills, and abilities for successful integration into leadership.[23]

Implementing Systems Thinking in Health Care

As previously discussed, the delivery of health care is enormously complex. New technology, devices, treatments, and lack of standardize practice have added to the complexity of care. Now more than ever, we need to identify clinical champions for systems thinking opportunities.[35] The key characteristics of systems thinkers are summarized in **BOX 3.5**.

Furthermore, to implement systems thinking in health care, we must have the support of the Board of Directors, the Chief Executive Officer, and other senior

---

BOX 3.5 Key Characteristics of a Health Systems Leader[31]

1. Acute awareness of the current system, knowing workflow process and best practice standards in the healthcare organization
2. Appreciation of the patterns and structures behind events
3. Willingness to challenge the current systems boundaries
4. Ability to speak to players at all levels of the hierarchy
5. Understanding of how relationships play out before making a decision
6. Conceptualization of the attributes of an improved and successful system
7. Processing of courage and energy to challenge the status quo and seek improvement

---

Trbovich P. Five ways to incorporate systems thinking into healthcare organizations. *Biomed Instrum Technol*. 2014; 48(s2): 31-36.

BOX 3.6 Five Ways to Incorporate Systems Thinking into Healthcare Organizations

1. Apply a holistic approach to solving problems: Seek a collective view (stakeholder involvement), identify the elements of the system, task dependencies, sequential sequencing order, coordination, and synchronization.
2. Define approaches for evaluating and understanding systems-wide effects.
3. Identify and nurture great systems thinkers.
4. Apply a proactive approach to identify leverage points.
5. Create a culture of systems thinking.

Trbovich P. Five ways to incorporate systems thinking into healthcare organizations. *Biomed Instrum Technol*. 2014; 48(s2): 31-36.

---

leaders. According to The Joint Commission standard LD.02.01, the primary responsibility of leaders is to provide for the safety and quality of care, treatment, and services.[36] Normally, this is defined in the hospital's mission, vision, and goals and clearly articulates how the hospital will achieve safety and quality.[36] The common purpose of the hospital must be embraced by all stakeholders. Trbovich provides five ways to incorporate systems thinking into healthcare organizations highlighted in **BOX 3.6**.[35]

The ultimate goal of the healthcare system is to produce better health outcomes for the population. Only when we take a systems approach to the delivery of care will we improve the healthcare environment, providing an exceptional patient experience that is safe with excellent quality outcomes at a reasonable cost. The time is now for all healthcare disciplines to embrace a systems thinking approach.[35]

▶ Interviews

Educator Interviews

Interview 3-1: An Interview with Undergraduate and Graduate Nurse Educators

Professor Barbara Keith, MSN, RN, CNE
Clinical Lecturer, School of Nursing
Vera Z. Dwyer College of Health Sciences, Indiana University, South Bend, Indiana
Dr. Teresa M. Dobrzykowski, RN, PhD, AGNP-BC
Assistant Dean and Graduate Program Director, School of Nursing & Associate Professor
Vera Z. Dwyer College of Health Sciences, Indiana University, South Bend, Indiana
Interviewed by Dr. Caren Rossow

What's your definition of systems thinking?

Professor Keith: Systems thinking is an ability and a mind-set to see beyond the one thing that is happening right in front of you and be able to learn how it interacts with everything else. It's kind of doing pattern recognition, to see patterns and then take it to the highest levels, to observe the bigger picture of outcomes, not just individual outcomes but population outcomes, because that is where systems thinking is going to lead you, eventually, beyond your patient to populations of patients, and then big population of patients. It's more like a mind-set, the willingness, and the ability to go beyond what your work is at this moment.

How do we progress beyond the work at the moment (individual patient care) to a systems thinking mind-set?

Professor Keith: That was the question I always had in my mind. Fifteen years ago, I first began to work with eight-semester nursing students who were getting ready to graduate. I tried to figure out why the "light bulb" goes on for some of them, they are able to see the bigger picture and yet, the "light bulb" never goes on for others. That became the basis for my research on critical thinking abilities and the criteria for critical thinking; most of it is a mind-set and not just looking at the simple answer. I did a longitudinal study of our nursing students, tested them at the beginning of our program using the California Critical Thinking Scale and then, at the end of the program. We did have a statistically significant change in critical thinking abilities and mind-set. It was a good sign, ensuring that they apply the critical thinking tendencies to healthcare delivery. The next step was when my colleagues and I joined a research study at Indiana University Purdue University Indianapolis (IUPUI) using simulation to measure critical thinking ability and clinical judgment. This research was led by Dr. Pam Jeffries at IUPUI, who is an expert in simulation learning. It was wonderful to be a part of this multi-campus study. It expanded my thinking to a larger level, exploring how to prepare our graduates to work in the healthcare system. How do I prepare them to think beyond patient care? This led to changes in our capstone course curriculum for our basic BSN students. We changed the way the course was delivered, adding complexity science, systems thinking, and simulation in the clinical setting.

How do you accomplish this in a clinical setting?

Professor Keith: We start by talking about the complexity and initially taking care of one patient, and then they gradually take on an RN staff assignment with an RN preceptor. Clinically, our instructors ask them to think beyond their patients: "What is going on in this organization right now that is impacting your ability to care for this patient? What complexities are creating these gaps in care that have the potential to hurt your patient? What can the RNs do within the system to bridge the gaps?" Like the Swiss Cheese model that allows accidents or never events to slip through the holes, we want our graduates to focus on the system and ways to improve care. It has been very successful, and our graduates in general are really prepared to systems think more than most new graduates.

How is systems thinking beneficial to the practice of nursing?

Professor Keith: Well, everything goes back to the IOM report, *To Err Is Human*. Other high-reliability organizations were way ahead of us in systems thinking; moving beyond the blame game. Nuclear energy organizations, the military, and air traffic control are good examples. High-reliability organizations have the potential for huge disasters several times a day, yet they are not having them. What are they doing that we are not? They did human error studies long before health care. When the *To Err Is Human* report was released, that's when health care started looking at the system and not the individual to blame. It's so amazing how little progress we have made. With all the initiatives, the IOM reports, The Joint Commission sentinel event alerts, we have made so little gain.

While students are in their eighth semester, we go over all the sentinel event alerts, why they are happening, where they are happening, how they are being reported, and the rates. Students are just shocked by this and cannot believe this is happening all the time in health care. So, they brainstorm why there is no change. Several have occurred in the perioperative area. There are limited systems thinking or interprofessional collaboration. A huge power differential remains and hopefully, the nurses we are graduating will be able to say, *"This is not the way we practice, this is not the way health care has to be."* Until somebody speaks up, it will never be fixed. One of the biggest issues we face is looking at health care simplistically or in a linear fashion. It is too complex to look at it this way. That is one reason why we have not made progress.

You have done a nice job in incorporating systems thinking into your capstone course. Although strides have been made, systems thinking has not been strongly adopted in other disciplines. How can we solve this? Interprofessional education (IPE) or interprofessional collaboration (IPC)?

Professor Keith: Unfortunately, I think a lot of the schools are doing IPE activities strictly to meet an accreditation requirement. It's not an integral part of what we do, it's a part that we check off. One of our colleagues, Dr. Lori Pajakowski, is collaborating with the IU School of Medicine to improve IPE and IPC. She has had very good success.

One of my RNs for her capstone project was working on communication between doctors and nurses. One of the patient floors she worked on was the premier unit for interdisciplinary rounds, but they stopped the practice. When it first started, it was wonderful. Over time, the residents stopped participating, so they don't have it any more, causing gaps in communication and concerns in the unit. For her capstone project, she is trying to restart the rounds in a way that is sustainable, hoping the residents will participate again because they see the benefit of the rounds and increased communication. However, the School of Medicine has to value it enough to have their residents participate. Are the doctors in charge of medical education on board doing interdisciplinary rounds? Are they going to support it and recognize the importance of it? Other health systems are practicing IPE, some are Magnet facilities and have been practicing multidisciplinary rounds for several years.

Dr. Dobrzykowski: Some have been Magnet facilities for up to 20 years, and they have great collaborative practice and outcomes. When you look at systems thinking, you need to look at the whole picture and definitely not linearly because it's spiral, circular, and ever changing. My theory would be Chaos theory.

Professor Keith: Or Complexity theory. Human error theory is so advanced. We are far behind the high-reliability organizations, as you mention. What is the problem? Part of it is the refusal or inability to recognize the complexity of health care. I think it's not only the inability to look at and recognize it, but it is the patriarchal system that occurred many years ago. The vestiges of the values and beliefs are embedded into health care. No one knows my discipline as well as I do. The residents come from different schools of medicine. We work with them on knowing and practicing IPE. Where does the gap occur? Does it come from their earlier preceptors–physicians? What do they value? It's a crucial breaking of the link. They may have had this in medical school but who are they precepting with and do they value the communication provided by others?

If you are a nurse providing care at the bedside, how can you incorporate systems thinking at this level?

Professor Keith: It is extremely hard. They are overwhelmed by being novices. When you are a novice, you put your blinders on as you have to do the medications and the dressing changes, and you have to be ready to report or they are going to think you are stupid. This whole mind-set, coming from the complexity theory and the research from Dr. Pat Ebright at IUPUI, is the idea that novices have "way more holes in their Swiss Cheese" than anyone else does. Because of that, their thinking becomes narrowed. As educators, we need to prepare them better, the preceptors need to be better educated, think out loud, and show the novices how their thought processes are working. Many times, they don't have enough staff, and then they experience nurses who lose their focus as all they can think about is task.

Dr. Dobrzykowski: They are tasked oriented.

You have the younger nurses seeking their nursing degree and those coming back for their BSNs whom you are teaching systems thinking. However, they get put into an environment with a diverse group of nurses and physicians who have no training in systems thinking.

Professor Keith: I think health care is doing better with looking at the root cause, the simple idea that an error is not one person's fault. They focus on the root cause analysis and, for the most part, find that poor communication is the cause every single time. The Joint Commission has shown this time and time again.

Dr. Dobrzykowski: It sits there as if we don't know what to do with it.

Professor Keith: They are not blaming, but the problems don't get fixed.

How has nursing education incorporated systems thinking into actual course work or clinical practicum?

Professor Keith: I have seen some immense changes in our RN to BSN program in their capstone projects. They have gone back to make significant changes in their organizations. Early in the RN to BSN program, I had three RNs who worked in the OR—the worst place for new graduates. They started the BSN program with a very narrow mind-set. I remember early in the program saying things like "The millennials just need to buck up, we are not going to hold their hands, if they can't handle us, they should not be in the operating room." By the time these RNs entered the capstone program, they were working on a program to retain nurses based on generational differences and the preceptor support model. The way they looked at things was so different. It was amazing. They take things back and make changes. We have not reached a critical mass. We have not reached the more experienced nurses, but I believe we are making a difference. They are much more focused on evidences.

What about the role of the nurse practitioner (NP)?

Dr. Dobryzkowski: First and foremost, we are NPs, we are always a nurse first, but our scope expands. There are certain things I do not do as an NP that a doctor does. There are blended things we do. But we are not physicians. It goes back to philosophy of the discipline. In those hierarchal models that value the discipline, it makes it very difficult, if not, almost impossible. When you look at the whole aspect of the linear hierarchal model versus a level playing field, all have our respected areas, all have our boundaries, but in some cases, we may cross over. After all, who was the original social worker? A nurse, a physical therapist (PT) , or an occupational therapist (OT)? You can say that of many of the different disciplines out there. Does that mean a nurse today can do the work of a PT? No, a PT has broadened and developed into its own discipline. Yes, we know how to turn patients every two hours, ambulate a patient, or transfer a patient. But to have me tell a patient how to do special exercises for an injury, that is beyond my scope of practice. We acknowledge this and tell that patient that the PT provider can take him or her further, to another level. It's a self-awareness of practice and also an appreciation of our boundaries, and it is ok to have these boundaries. This is my scope of practice, this is the other discipline's scope of practice, and we may have some crossover. It's within the common areas where we can work together. For example, can pharmacists give shots? Yes, they receive the same level of education, and they can learn to give shots. Yes, they can give them as well as nurses. But what about those things nurses do? What about some of the things nurses know better? Functional status? Maximizing a multiple sclerosis patient's potential by helping the patient with scheduled medications and with activities to combat fatigue is how nurses think. The nurse collaborates with the pharmacist to better understand when to take the medications to maximize effect and incorporates this into the plan of care. How do we give medications to minimize fatigue? Then, the PT works on the patient's fatigue, and when to work with the patient is coordinated with the information from the pharmacist. When is the best time for the patient to do physical therapy? Maybe a change in exercises is in order to decrease the fatigue—less energy expending. It's comfortable knowing one's limitations and this awareness is comforting. Outcomes in our program are always there—in collaboration with course outcomes and program outcomes. The NP program is designed as systems thinking model and as one of collaborative practice with all disciplines, the patient, family, and their culture. We can make this a demand of our graduate students because they have an understanding of nursing; however, our undergrads are overwhelmed and need to focus on the patient first before they can expand into systems thinking. We as faculty need to model and mentor.

It comes back to our discipline: We are holistic thinkers. We look at different models and scenarios, trying to collaborate and systems think.

How have you incorporated systems thinking into your graduate course work in the NP program?

Dr. Dobrzykowski: We begin to incorporate it by IPE and IPC into the system of care. We were one of the first groups to get our students involved with the IU School of Medicines IPE program. I think our problem is not as convoluted with the semesters as the undergraduate programs. We also have great faculty buy in. Because of our provider role, most of us still practice and we also teach. So, we see that collaboration is vital in our practices. Without collaboration, where would we be? Where would our patients and our families be without collaboration? As NPs, our certification has practice requirements that force us to keep current, and it maintains a constant mind-set of collaboration. It's a part of us, as much as breathing is. If you look at the original NP models, you note that we have a cohesive team with physicians, a collaborative practice. In many states, NPs are moving toward or have an independent practice. Here in Indiana, we are moving toward having them work collaboratively for their first years, where they are mentored by either an experienced NP or MD/DO, and then perhaps they can later become established in independent practice. Even for new physicians coming out, they have a learning curve. This is not meant to be punitive in nature but mentoring is critical. Fostering communication and teamwork. This is not competitive.

Why do you believe systems thinking has not easily been adopted in health care?

Professor Keith: Part of it is the silos we learned in. If we had true IPE, not to just check off a box but a genuine effort to try to understand each other, then we could move forward. Complexity theorists would say that it's because we don't recognize the complexity of health care and that we continue to try to solve problems in a linear fashion. We are not systems thinking. The resources are so strained now in health care, everyone seems to be in survival mode. When you're in survival mode, you are not thinking about systems thinking.

Dr. Dobrzykowski: I agree with everything that Professor Keith has said. We have a political system that is currently unfriendly to health care. We don't know what is happening with the Affordable Care Act. There are fears about not having medical homes, which is collaboration at its best. This type of primary care model is being threatened. So, we are in survival mode. Every provider and discipline are in it for themselves. Instead of working together, we start fighting for the scarce resources. Even in areas where there has been collaboration, we are seeing a narrower focus.

Dr. Dobrzykowski: What does society expect out of healthcare workers? Health care is the least exact science, but we are the ones who need exactness. People are different and how they react is different; it's the human condition. When you teach differential diagnosis and clinical reasoning, it truly can be an educated guest based on the evidence at hand. Many times, we are spot on, many times we are close, and many times we miss the boat completely. Our patients and our American culture expect the physician to do no wrong and always be the head of something. Our society puts physicians on pedestals, and we expect them to know and always have a cure. That's a huge amount of responsibility, and for many physicians, it's one of the ways to close in and hold on, too, as I am supposed to do this. The other difficulty is: It is hard to say that you don't know when society expects you to know. When you talk about interprofessional collaboration and systems thinking, you are open to others' views. It's like the iceberg model. This is what you see, the many patterns, but below the water are all the values and beliefs that impact the system. How much of what we do is driven by our underlying value and beliefs? Every action we have is driven by these values.

Dr. Dobrzykowski: There must be a change in culture in order to have systems thinking. In making change, you will have people who want to make the change and others will want to know what is in it for them. You can come easy and are loved or if you don't, there are consequences. … pay perhaps? There must be some acknowledgment and respect of the evidence for change. Research clearly shows how to decrease mortality and morbidity. Units that have better educated nurses, adequate staff, and nurse autonomy produce better outcomes with notable decreases in mortality and morbidity. We must tie outcomes to collaboration and payment. It's a much better carrot. At the same time, we need to stop lumping in nurses as part of environmental services or part of the hotel industry and start to see them as professionals. Even from a fee structure, most systems include nursing services in the hotel or room fee. We need to stop seeing nurses as expenditures but as assets providing safe cost-effective care in an error-free environment. There must be a change in culture to recognize the contribution of nursing. Actually, we need to recognize the contribution of all disciplines. If they work together, then you have a barrier that is broken, ease in communication, collaboration, leading to decreased length of hospital stay, decreased mortality and morbidity, and increased patient satisfaction. When the barriers are broken, then we can systems think.

How can we create a systems thinking culture in health care?

Professor Keith: I believe resources have to be tied to collaborative practices.

Dr. Dobrzykowski: Yes.

Professor Keith: In other words, you don't get as much reimbursement from the Center for Medicare and Medicaid Services (CMS). All disciplines need to practice IPE or they receive less reimbursement. You have to tie it to resources. You will always have some great doctors and nurses who are truly committed to improving health care and they are onboard for systems thinking. However, you have those who will have to have the carrot or the stick.

Dr. Dobrzykowski: Look at the reward they get for practicing in health care. For some, it is very internal, for doing the right thing, whereas for others, it could be financial. If I don't do this, then I will lose reimbursement.

Professor Keith: Right now, the hospitals are losing their reimbursement. Providers who don't or won't change their practice style should be losing their reimbursement.

Dr. Dobrzykowski: Or be fined. Providers (in all disciplines) not only in the acute care system, the entire continuum of care, including PT and OT. Medicine seems to be the most siloed. It begins with training. Most are trained in the Cartesian model of care. How can you expect them to systems think? Their roots are not in systems thinking. Nurses training is much different, to think holistically.

Professor Keith: Tying collaboration into payment will help. Indicators were developed for meaningful use and CMS surely can develop them for collaboration.

Dr. Dobrzykowski: This may help stop the blame game and move us forward toward collaborative practice, a just culture, and a systems thinking approach to health care.

Interview 3-2: Clinical Systems Thinker Interview

Interview with Naomi DeShore

Nurse Practitioner, Walter Reed Medical Center

Washington, DC

What's your definition of systems thinking?

Ms. DeShore: It's kind of a conglomerate. I form a visual picture in my mind with the macro- and the microlevels that constitute my system. At the macrolevel, I have the large Veterans Administration and the Department of Defense, and my microlevel is my small unit. However, I service 26 other departments, so I have 26 bubbles (**FIGURE 3.3**) with arrows at both ends, going out and coming in. Everything has to go out and in because of the interrelationship and the interdependence I have with these other departments. Systems thinking is how I recognize, understand, and synthesize my unit's interrelationships and interdependencies.

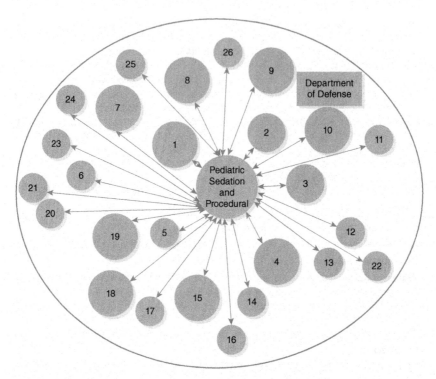

FIGURE 3.3 Systems Drawing Pediatric Sedation and Procedural Unit Domain

I have arrows going in and out of my little bubbles. It's one big bubble with lots of little bubbles!

It's a holistic approach for looking at the healthcare system. It allows us to do a focused analysis of the system, of its constituent parts, and again, how they are interrelated, and how they work over time and within the context of the system. Within the macrolevel, I like to think of how I do something and at the microlevel, I do what it takes to get it done. We need to look at it from different ways, through the management lenses. How does culture impact the system? You must look at the culture, the power structure, and the strategic design of the organization when you are looking at this picture. You just cannot say we are going to do systems thinking. You may have to tag it to things that are getting done, so people have an understanding.

How is systems thinking beneficial to the practice of nursing?

Ms. DeShore: I think it's holistic and overall, it optimizes patient care. It leads to collaboration and patient-centered care. But at my institution, it is patient- and family-centered care. It's what we have to think about. Families are an important component, especially in my work because I take care of children. Children don't just walk into an institution; their family members bring them. They care for them.

Collaboration fosters teamwork, quality, and safety. I think we do fairly well in quality, but not in safety. The statistics certainly support this. For nurses, systems thinking allows them to improve their problem-solving skills and make good decisions and enables them to interact with other professionals on an individual level. As they learn systems thinking, they can better optimize the patient's environment and care.

In what ways can you apply systems thinking to actual clinical practice?

Ms. DeShore: By my visual bubbles with arrows. My macro is the Department of Defense and those 26 bubbles I serve, the Army, the Navy, and the children of the military in Europe, who come to Walter Reed as transfers. We are the tertiary center for the eastern portion of the seaboard. Our pediatric center is separated from adult care. Whatever care is needed, the pediatric patient is in one location. For example, if they are coming in for an invasive procedure, the pre-procedure screen, sedation, procedure, and post-procedure recovery are all done in one area. They are managed by pediatric providers. We also provide education for noninvasive procedures as well as play therapy and other care. We choose to separate for safety. We have limited the number of people who can administer sedation. The old Army Walter Reed merged into the new Navy Walter Reed in 2011. At the old Walter Reed, we had difficulty keeping people competent and we had medication errors. We did not have good outcomes, so now with our new unit, we focus just on pediatrics and we have had zero negative outcomes. We changed the system with standardized process, procedures, medications, and documentation, leaving little room for error. We have put in place the right structure to minimize error. My micro is my department.

In this high-risk environment, have you taken away the high-risk practices by standardizing everything you are doing based on best-practice?

Ms. DeShore: Yes, we limit the number of patients to ensure we can provide great care. One nurse takes care of one patient. No one floats into our area. The Joint Commission came in and lauded us for our processes. There have been no errors and no use of reversal agents in 10 years. No never events! We don't cross the line. We did this because we are a military system that is not always child friendly. When we moved from the old hospital, we moved the Department of Pediatrics to the new hospital. They never had inpatient pediatrics or a moderate sedation unit. They only had clinics. We injected a whole new children's world within an adult environment.

Why do you believe systems thinking has not easily been adopted in health care?

Ms. DeShore: I never realized I was doing systems thinking until I was in my Doctorate of Health Administration program, Dr. Johnson's class. Yet, I have a Bachelor's and two Master's degrees. I myself have been involved in ongoing education. It is not something that is spoken of. I think the new generation of nurse practitioners get it, they understand what it is. But for all of us, systems thinking will not be there until we get into a leadership position and it can help educate and filter it down. Then, it will happen. I think one of the issues is that many feel like it is just another quality initiative they want us to do. In the Air Force, we had Total Force Quality and several other quality programs. It's just a new package with a new phrase; it's not going to stick. Because in performance improvement, we talk about root cause analysis versus looking at the one problem versus looking at it from a systems thinking approach. They want a root cause analysis, so what are you going to do with the root? What about everything else that goes with it? So, I give you the root and the plant dies. Unless you are participating in ongoing education or advancing yourself, it is not going to come. Even the education department in my hospital is unaware of systems thinking. To just say we are going to do systems thinking and incorporate it into clinical practice is not a concept in this organization. So, until we see a new generation of nurses and practitioners graduating, we are not going to see it. They are going to be the integrators. I don't believe it will happen in my organization. When I was in my Master's of Public Administration program, we learned to look at healthcare organizations from different lenses. You have the political, strategic, and cultural. What is the cultural lens of the organization? If you are in my organization, you are going to walk in, be quiet, and sit. However, there are a number of very progressive organizations out there where nurses can hit the floor running. They are mentored and grown. So, I believe it is dependent on the culture of the organization.

How can we create a systems thinking culture in health care?

Ms. DeShore: You must look at the philosophy, the culture of the organization. However, many organizations have little collaboration. Systems thinking would never work in my facility. Part of it is the organization, and the other part is the annual staff change (1/3 of the staff). The medical service chiefs, deputy directors, and directors of nursing change, and new administrators come in with their own set of ideas on how they want things done. There is no consistency. The up and coming healthcare providers will need to promote systems thinking, for example, hopefully, those who go back for additional education, like the RN to BSN or those going for their Master's degree or doctorate. I believe it needs to start at the educational level but also within organizations. Interdisciplinary education and collaboration will help. For example, at the old Walter Reed, when we had safety errors, we began our safety huddles that were interdisciplinary; we collaborated to look at patient safety and quality issues. It was open to anyone who would like to come. Once we started this, things really changed on how people felt about pediatrics. Quality and safety were the focus, but other things grew out of this. Providers began to understand why and how other disciplines practice, and why they do the things they do. It was like a huge love fest in the end. Even though these were serious issues, it allowed providers who do not understand pediatrics the opportunity to learn. Like the pharmacist who does not do pediatrics, why is dosing so important? Or when we ask for a specific drug, why do we want it? You must have a starting point. Some organizations have embraced interprofessional education and collaboration, whereas others see it as the new buzz word. In the military, you have frequent change of Chief Executive Officers, 2 years army, 2 years navy. Then, you have deployments, assignment of new duties, with personnel leaving and new personnel coming. There is constant change, which makes us more reactive than proactive. It makes it difficult.

The culture, empowering people, and strategic design of the organization need systems thinking plugged in. It has to start from the top down. You have to believe it can be adopted. Leadership has to understand the complexity of the healthcare system. That is something we have not done. Our U.S. healthcare system is so complex. We can plug systems thinking into the microlevel, but how do we plug it into the macrolevel? Consider the complexity of the social systems, the family, and everything else that goes along with it. After all, we cannot get health insurance right, so how can we do this? How many decades have we been trying to figure this out? It's complex.

References

1. Institute of Medicine. To err is human: building a safer health system. Nationalacademies. org. http://www.nationalacademies.org/hmd/~/media/Files/Report%20Files/1999/To-Err-is -Human/To%20Err%20is%20Human%201999%20%20report%20brief.pdf. Published November, 1999:1-8. Accessed January 18, 2018.
2. Institute of Medicine. Crossing the quality chasm: a new health system for the 21st century. Nationalacademies.org. http://www.nationalacademies.org/hmd/~/media/Files/Report%20 Files/2001/Crossing-the-Quality-Chasm/Quality%20Chasm%202001%20%20report%20 brief.pdf. Published March, 2001:1-8. Accessed January 18, 2018.
3. The Joint Commission. Jointcommission.org. Facts about the national patient safety goals. https://www.jointcommission.org/facts_about_the_national_patient_safety_goals/. Published December, 28, 2017:Para. 1–4. Accessed February 10, 2018.
4. VA National Center for Patient Safety. VA.gov. TIPS Special Edition: JCAHO Patient Safety Goals 2003. https://www.patientsafety.va.gov/docs/TIPS/TIPSDec02.pdf. Published December, 2002:1-10. Accessed February 12, 2018.
5. ECRI Institute. Ecri.org. Joint Commission Updates Sentinel Event Statistics. https://www .ecri.org/components/HRCAlerts/Pages/HRCAlerts111815_Joint.aspx. Published November 18, 2015. Accessed March 24, 2018.

6. Berwick DM, Calkins DR, McCannon CJ, Hackbarth AD. The 100,000 lives campaign: setting a goal and a deadline for improving health care quality. *JAMA*. 2006;295(3):324-327.

7. Institute for Healthcare Improvement. Ihi.org. Overview of the 100,000 campaign. http://www.ihi.org/engage/initiatives/completed/5millionlivescampaign/documents/overview%20of%20the%20100k%20campaign.pdf. Published n.d., 1-2. Accessed February 1, 2018.

8. Baehrend J. 100,000 lives campaign, ten years later. http://www.ihi.org/communities/blogs/_layouts/15/ihi/community/blog/ItemView.aspx?List=7d1126ec-8f63-4a3b-9926-c44ea3036813&ID=268&Web=1e880535-d855-4727-a8c1-27ee672f115d. Published June 17, 2016. Accessed February 12, 2018.

9. Institute for Healthcare Improvement. Ihi.org. Initiatives: overview protecting 5 million lives from harm. http://www.ihi.org/Engage/Initiatives/Completed/5MillionLivesCampaign/Pages/default.aspx . Published 2018. Accessed February 12, 2018.

10. Institute for Healthcare Improvement. Ihi.org Initiatives. IHI triple aim initiative. http://www.ihi.org/Engage/Initiatives/TripleAim/Pages/default.aspx. Published 2018. Accessed March 28, 2018.

11. Leap Frog Group Hospital Safety Grade. Hospital Errors are the Third Leading Cause of Death in U.S., and New Hospital Safety Scores Show Improvements Are Too Slow. http://www.hospitalsafetygrade.org/newsroom/display/hospitalerrors-thirdleading-causeofdeathinus-improvementstooslow. Published October 23, 2013. Accessed January 15, 2018.

12. Safety Improves, but Crucial Work Remains. http://www.leapfroggroup.org/news-events/five-years-after-launch-leapfrog-hospital-safety-grade-patient-safety-improves-crucial. Published April 12, 2017. Accessed January 15, 2018.

13. Dolansky MA, Moore SM. Quality and Safety Education for Nurses (QSEN): the key is systems thinking. *Online J Issues Nurs*. 2013;18(3):1-12.

14. Plack MM, Goldman EF, Scott AR, et al. Systems thinking and systems-based practice across the health professions: an inquiry into definitions, teaching practices, and assessment. *Teach Learn Med*. 2017;28:1-13.

15. Norman CD. Teaching systems thinking and complexity theory in health sciences. *J Eval Clin Pract*. 2013;19:1087-1089.

16. Moore SM, Dolansky MA, Singh M, Palmieri P, Alemi F, The Systems Thinking Scale. Case western reserve university. https://case.edu/nursing/media/nursing/pdf-dox/STS_Manual.pdf. Published March 2011:1-27. Accessed February 12, 2018.

17. Phillips JM, Staltler AM, Dolansky MA, McKee Lopez G. Fostering future leadership in quality and safety through systems thinking. *J Prof Nurs*. 2016;32(1):15-24.

18. QSEN. Competencies.qsen.org. http://qsen.org/competencies. Published 2003. Accessed January 3, 2018.

19. QSEN. Project overview: the evolution of the quality and safety education for nurses (QSEN) initiative. http://qsen.org/about-qsen/project-overview/. Published 2012. Accessed January 3, 2018.

20. Staltler AM, Mota AM. Recommendations for promoting quality and safety in health care systems. *J Contin Educ Nurs*. 2017;48(7):295-297.

21. Future of Nursing Campaign for Action. Dashboard Indicators. https://campaignforaction.org/wp-content/uploads/2017/07/Dash-1e.png. Published. August 7, 2017. Accessed March 10, 2018.

22. Institute of Medicine. Nationalacademies.org. The future of nursing: leading change, advancing health. http://nationalacademies.org/hmd/reports/2010/the-future-of-nursing-leading-change-advancing-health.aspx. Published October 5, 2010. Accessed March 27, 2018.

23. Johnson JA, Rossow CC. *Health Organizations: Theory, Behavior, and Development*. Burlington, MA: Jones & Bartlett Learning; 2019.

24. Millinger A, Brennan L, Schoenfelder T. Calipper whitepaper: chief nursing executive leadership analysis report. Caliper Corporation. http://www.calipermedia.calipercorp.com/whitepapers/us/Chief-Nursing-Executives-Leadership-Analysis-Report.pdf. Published 2011. Accessed March 3, 2018.

25. Spurgeon P, Flanagan H, Cooke M, Sujan M, Cross S, Jarvis R. Creating a safer health system: lessons from other sectors and an account of an application in the safer clinical systems programme. *Health Serv Manage Res*. 2017;30(2):85-93.

26. Luanaigh P, Hughes F. The nurse executive role in quality and high performing health services. *J Nurs Manage [serial online]*. January 2016;24(1):132-136. Available from: CINAHL Plus with Full Text, Ipswich, MA. Accessed March 2, 2018.

27. Tetuan T, Ohm R, Kinzie L, McMaster S, Moffitt B, Mosier M. Does systems thinking improve the perception of safety culture and patient safety? *J Nurs Regul*. 2017;8(2):31-39.

28. Marmor J. Systems thinking is psychiatry: some theoretical and clinical implications. *Am J Psychiatry*. 1983;140(7):833-838.

29. Fogarty CT, Mauksch LB. Imaging a clinical world without family systems thinking. *Families, Syst Health*. 2017;35(4):395-398.

30. Sturmberg JP, Martin CM, Katerndahl DA. Systems and complexity thinking in the general practice literature: an integrative, historical narrative review. *Ann Fam Med*. 2014;12(1):66-74.

31. Guralnick S, Ludwig S, Englander R. Domain of competence: systems-based practice. *Acad Pediatr*. 2014;14(2 Suppl):S70-S79.

32. Johnson JK, Miller SH, Horowitz SD. Systems-based practice: improving the safety and quality of patient care by recognizing and improving the systems in which we work and live. ahrq.org. https://www.ahrq.gov/downloads/pub/advances2/vol2/Advances-Johnson_90.pdf Published 2010:1-10. Accessed January 30, 2018.

33. Colbert CY, Myers JD, Cable CT, et al. An alternative practice model: residents transform community clinic and become systems thinkers. *J Grad Med Educ*. 2012;4(2):232-236.

34. Gillen JR, Ramirez AG, Fairneau DW, et al. Using interdisciplinary workgroups to educate surgery residents in systems-based practice. *J Surg Educ*. 2016;73(6):1052-1059.

35. Trbovich P. Five ways to incorporate systems thinking into healthcare organizations. *Biomed Instrum Technol*. 2014;48(s2):31-36.

36. The Joint Commission. *Advancing Effective Communication, Cultural Competence, and Patient-and Family-Centered Care: A Roadmap for Hospitals*. Oakbrook Terrace, IL: The Joint Commission; 2010:1-102.

CHAPTER 4

Systems Thinking for Public and Global Health

▶ Public Health and Population Health Perspectives

Fundamentally, public health consists of organized efforts to improve the health of human populations.[1] Critical in this definition is the focus; public health efforts are directed to populations rather than to individuals. Public health does not rely on a narrow or specific body of knowledge and expertise but rather on a dynamic, multidisciplinary approach that often combines social sciences, medical sciences, and natural sciences. Public health scholar Richard Riegelman, in his expansion of the public health definition to include the even broader concept of population health, offers the following definition:

> The totality of all evidence-based public and private efforts to preserve and promote health and prevent disease, disability, and death.[2]

In their book *Public Health Administration: Principles of Population-Based Management*, Shi and Johnson describe the scope of public health, using a population health framework, which includes the full range of physical, environmental, social, and economic determinants of health plus the full range of interventions that address health issues, including the structure and function of health systems and the role of health policy[1] (**FIGURE 4.1**).

The Institute of Medicine (IOM) in its impactful report *The Future of Public Health* similarly defined public health as an "organized community effort to address the public interest in health by applying scientific and technical knowledge to prevent disease and promote health."[3] From a systems perspective, which aligns well with the population–health framework, public health is described by medical social scientist James Johnson as follows: "Public health is highly interconnected and interdependent in its relationship to individuals, communities, and the larger society, including the global community. Using the language of systems theory, public health is a complex adaptive system. It is complex in that it is composed of multiple,

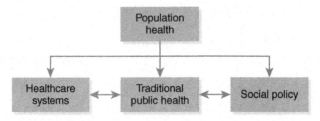

FIGURE 4.1 Population Health Framework

BOX 4.1 The NCI Statement on Systems Thinking

Public health researchers and practitioners often work to solve complex population and health issues, such as obesity and chronic disease, which are deeply embedded within the fabric of society. As such, the solutions often require intervention and engagement with key stakeholders and organizations across many levels ranging from local entities (schools, churches, and work environments) to regional systems (health departments and hospital networks) to entire countries (national agencies). This multilevel, multiparticipant view is at the heart of systems thinking, a process of understanding how parts influence one another within a whole.

Reproduced from National Cancer Institute, Washington, DC. Available at: https://researchtoreality.cancer.gov.

---

diverse, interconnected elements, and it is adaptive in that the system is capable of changing and learning from experience and its environment."[4]

Furthermore, the systems approach in public health is more than the relationships that support and facilitate the organization and actions of public health but also includes "the mind-set" of public health professionals—thus, systems thinking. The National Cancer Institute (NCI), one of the first public health agencies to embrace systems thinking, found it a useful paradigm in their Tobacco Control efforts. Their statement on systems thinking for health is shown in **BOX 4.1**.

Systems Thinking as Core Pubic Health Competency

The Association of Schools of Public Health identifies systems thinking as a core competency in their Health Policy and Management domain for the education of public health professionals.[1] By looking at the core functions of public health and the essential services, we can see a role for systems thinking throughout. The graphic provided in **FIGURE 4.2** identifies the essential services while also demonstrating the importance of placing public health in the systems context. The center ring in the diagram is labeled "system management," and it interlocks with all of the services, thus interconnectivity. Outside of the essential services in the diagram is arrows that demonstrate the cyclical nature of the core functions identified by the IOM: (1) assessment, (2) policy development, and (3) assurance.

Assessment involves obtaining data to define the health of populations and the nature of health problems. This process is ongoing and continuous because of new challenges or changes in health determinants.

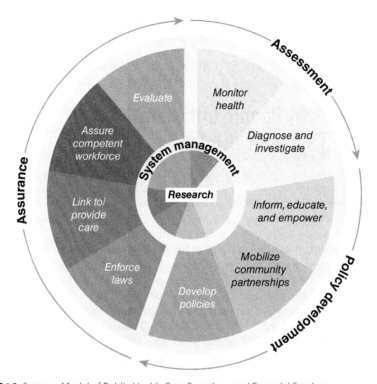

FIGURE 4.2 Systems Model of Public Health Core Functions and Essential Services

Reproduced from Centers for Disease Control and Prevention, National Public Health Performance Standards Program: Orientation to the Essential Public Health Services. Available at: htttp://www.cdc.gov/nphpsp/essentialServices.html. Accessed on March 25, 2012.

Assurance includes the oversight responsibility for ensuring that essential components of an effective health system are in place. A continuous process involves many feedback loops.

Policy development includes developing evidence-based recommendations and analyses to guide public policy as it pertains to health. This is best done within a systems model.

To further explore the influence of systems thinking, we can look at one of these core functions, *policy development*, using systems language and perspectives. Health policy expert Walter Jones describes the following three policy system characteristics[1]:

Complexity. Numerous influences interact to produce a system that is continually in flux while generally attaining some level of equilibrium or stability. Individuals, interest groups, organizations, and communities are all actors in the policy process.

Interrelatedness. Most significant activities are connected to one another by feedback loops, with direct and indirect impacts. All policy actions create reactions within the system, some even modifying the system itself.

Cyclical processes. With complexity and interrelatedness, the policy process does not have a definite beginning or end, but it continues on as long as the society continues to exist. There are no permanent policy successes or failures, just a continual cycle.

One way in which public health policy gains influence in the larger society is through long range systemic planning. This, too, is shaped by systems thinking, as you will see in the sections on national health goals in the United States (*Healthy People 2020*) and global goals set by the United Nations (*Sustainable Development Goals 2030*).

▶ Healthy People Initiatives and Systems Thinking

The U.S. Department of Health and Human Services, in collaboration with community partners, develops 10-year plans outlining certain key national health and health-related objectives to be accomplished during each subsequent decade since 1980. The current mission is as follows: "*Healthy People 2020*" strives to: (1) identify nationwide health improvement priorities; (2) increase public awareness and understanding of the determinants of health, disease, and disability and the opportunities for progress; (3) provide measurable objectives and goals that can be used at national, state, and local levels; (4) engage multiple sectors to take actions that are driven by the best available evidence and knowledge; and (5) identify critical research and data collection needs. Moving forward "*Health People 2030*" mission is to guide the United States in achieving its' full potential for health and well-being so that it is second to none among developed countries. **FIGURE 4.3** presents a systems model that incorporates determinants of health and the range of conditions influencing health. You will see at the center of the model individual characteristics, including biological factors with concentric rings extending out from there expanding to include social, cultural, economic, and environmental conditions at the local,

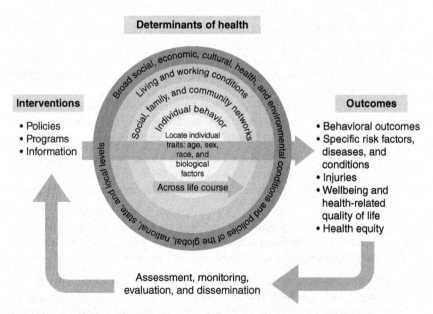

FIGURE 4.3 Systems Model of *Healthy People Initiatives*
Reproduced from the Department of Health and Human Services.

state, national, and global levels. If you follow the arrows in the model, you will see public health interventions in the form of policies, programs, and information that must cut across all of these to achieve the desired outcomes, and even then, as explained earlier by Jones and shown by the arrows, will be cyclical.

To be more comprehensive in looking at social and health systems as a whole, *Healthy People 2020* is differentiated from previous Healthy People initiatives by including multiple new areas in its objective list, such as adolescent health, blood disorders, and blood safety; dementias; genomics; global health; healthcare-associated infections; quality of life and well-being; lesbian, gay, bisexual, and transgender health; older adults; preparedness; sleep health; and social determinants of health. From the preliminary work on *Healthy People 2030*, we can anticipate an even further evolution of systems thinking for the development and achievement of the next decade of national health goals and objectives.

▶ Sustainable Development Goals (SDGs) and Systems Thinking

The SDGs are a new, universal set of goals, targets, and indicators that UN member states will be expected to use to frame their agendas and political policies over the next 15 years. The SDGs came into effect in January 2016, and they will continue to guide United Nations Development Program (UNDP) policy and funding until 2030. As the lead UN development agency, UNDP is uniquely placed to help implement the goals through our work in some 170 countries and territories.

Eight health-related goals of the 17 SDGs are:

- GOAL 1: No Poverty
- GOAL 2: Zero Hunger
- GOAL 3: Good Health and Well-Being
- GOAL 4: Quality Education
- GOAL 5: Gender Equality
- GOAL 6: Clean Water and Sanitation
- GOAL 7: Affordable and Clean Energy
- GOAL 8: Decent Work and Economic Growth

These goals build on the successes of the Millennium Development Goals, while including new areas such as climate change, economic inequality, innovation, sustainable consumption, peace, and justice, among other priorities. Concurrent with the systems thinking perspective, the goals are **interconnected**—often, the key to success on one will involve tackling issues more commonly associated with another. They serve to identify and address **root causes** while uniting people for positive change. The UNDP provides support to governments to integrate the SDGs into their national development plans and policies, including health systems and public health. The track record **working across multiple goals** to achieve system-wide improvements increases the likelihood of reaching the targets set out in the SDGs by 2030. Partnerships among all stakeholders: Governments, private sector, civil society/Nongovernmental Organizations (NGOs), and citizens will continue to be a critical success factor. The area of health is multi-sectoral, highly interconnected, and has challenges with many root causes. Both achievements and challenges are shown in **BOX 4.2**.

BOX 4.2 SDG Goal 3: Good Health and Well-Being

We have made huge strides in reducing child mortality, improving maternal health, and fighting HIV/AIDS, malaria, and other diseases. Since 1990, there has been globally an over 50% decline in preventable child deaths. Maternal mortality also fell by 45% worldwide. New HIV/AIDS infections decreased by 30% between 2000 and 2013, and over 6.2 million lives were saved from malaria.

Despite this incredible progress, more than 6 million children still die before their fifth birthday every year. Approximately 16,000 children die each day from preventable diseases such as measles and tuberculosis. Every day, hundreds of women die during pregnancy or from childbirth-related complications. In many rural areas, only 56% of births are attended by skilled professionals. AIDS is now the leading cause of death among teenagers in sub-Saharan Africa, a region still severely devastated by the HIV epidemic.

These deaths can be avoided through prevention and treatment, education, immunization campaigns, and sexual and reproductive health care. The SDGs make a bold commitment to end the epidemics of AIDS, tuberculosis, malaria, and other communicable diseases by 2030. The aim is to achieve universal health coverage and provide access to safe and affordable medicines and vaccines for all. Supporting research and development for vaccines is an essential part of this process as well.

Reproduced from United Nations Development Program (UNDP). Available at: http://www.undp.org/content/undp/en/home/sustainable-development-goals/goal-3-good-health-and-well-being.html.

Furthermore, SDG 3: Health and Well-Being provides a good example of how systems thinking can be utilized and can serve to integrate action across the 17 goals, as illustrated in **FIGURE 4.4**.

To elaborate further on the importance of systems thinking for the successful achievement of the SDGs, the *Forum for the Future* cautions that we must always keep systems thinking at the fore. The Forum's Chief Change Officer Stephanie Draper asserts:

Systems thinking identifies the interactions between different parts of a system—a city, a society, a sector—and ensures they deliver more than the sum of the parts. In today's world, we're pretty good at setting goals and then slavishly working to achieve them. But if the SDGs are really going to shift our whole system onto a sustainable path, we need serious amounts of joined-up thinking that goes deeper to address underlying causes. Successfully delivering the SDGs requires a really strong systems approach. For organizations rising to the challenge, that means operating on *three levels*—joining up with others' efforts to achieve individual goals; looking at the inter-relationships between all the goals; and finally delivering the goals in a way that models the characteristics we need for a sustainable society.[5]

These three levels of systems change that necessitate a systems thinking mindset for professionals, policy leaders, and ultimately for the entire global community are summarized in **BOX 4.3**.

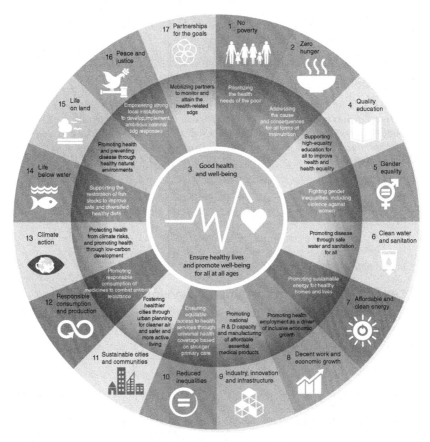

FIGURE 4.4 Health and Well-Being Interconnection with All SDGs

Health in The SDG Era. Reproduced with permission from World Health Organization.

BOX 4.3 Levels of Systems Change Needed for Achieving Global Goals

Level 1: Joined-up efforts on individual goals

How are we ensuring that the combined activities across the world add up to more than the sum of their parts?

CAVEAT: A failure to see interconnections across and within the goals could lead to activity that misses the opportunity of synergistic effort.

NEEDED: Identify what the system is actually for, where the interlinkages are, and who holds the power, resources, and innovations that work for or against change. Understanding the system in detail means we can find and unlock the most powerful opportunities for significant shifts (the nutritional quality of soil, for example, underpins the whole food system). But the vital next step is to work collectively with others to better understand the wider system they are all aiming to fix—be it the global food system, or health and well-being for all—and find the best points of leverage.

(continues)

BOX 4.3 Levels of Systems Change Needed for Achieving
Global Goals *(continued)*

Level 2: A "network set" of goals

*What are the interrelationships across the goals? How can we understand the
different drivers and root causes of a number of different goals regionally,
nationally, and globally? Which goals work together to deliver a change in a system,
and how do we make the most of those combinations? Where are the tensions
between them?*

CAVEAT: Here, we have to guard against remaining in our professional and policy silos.

NEEDED: Mapping the activities around the individual goals to accelerate progress
is needed. But also looking across the goals at possible synergies is essential.
Clearly, the SDGs do not work in isolation—health (SDG 3) is impacted by food and
nutrition, sanitation, education, and increasingly climate change. At a minimum, as
the UN reviews progress against each goal, they should not just track metrics but
interrelationships between them and the learning.

Level 3: The "how" of sustainable development

*How are we addressing the SDGs? What are the underlying principles that will drive
success?*

CAVEAT: If today's global system was working really well for everyone, we would not
need to set goals for ending poverty and hunger. The current system is not set up with
sustainable development in mind, so it risks consistently undermining our efforts.

NEEDED: Leverage points for systems change, including shifting the goals of whole
systems, as the SDGs have done; changing the mind-set or mental models of
stakeholders; and organizing as systems and systems within systems. That means being
inclusive in the activities that are developed, and in their governance, it means naming
the assumptions being made about what will work and in what context, and finally, it
means getting serious about a systems thinking mind-set that values people taking
control of their own future.

Modified by J. Johnson from Forum for the Future website https://www.forumforthefuture.org/blog/systems-thinking-unlocking
-sustainable-development-goals. Accessed April 5, 2018.

▶ Systems Thinking at the World Health Organization (WHO)

The very definition of health found in the WHO's 1948 Constitution is based on
a systems perspective: "Health is a state of complete physical, mental, and social
well-being …." A decade ago, the WHO published a report titled *Systems Thinking for Health Systems Strengthening*, in which they claimed systems thinking is a
"paradigm shift" for public and global health.[1,6] As stated, "Systems thinking offers
a more comprehensive way of anticipating synergies and mitigating negative emergent behaviors, with direct relevance for creating more system-ready policies."[6] They
advocated the understanding and adoption of systems thinking within their own
organization, as well as in their multitude of collaborative public health projects

throughout the world. In fact, the WHO promotes the systems thinking approach in Ministries of Health worldwide using health systems building blocks. Furthermore, by advocating "Health in All Policies," as described in **BOX 4.4**, the WHO serves as a catalyst to get Ministries in all areas of government to work with the Health Ministry to address the public health implications and potential unintended consequences that affect the health of individuals, communities, and the nation.

For example, the Ministry of Agriculture (or the Department of Agriculture) would engage the Health Ministry (in the United States, it is the Department of Health and Human Services) in their policy development process, as would the Transportation Ministry (Department of Transportation). One can see many opportunities in each of these for health promotion and prevention; food security and road safety are two common examples. A strong case for this will be presented in the section titled *One Health*.

Additionally, the WHO hosts the Alliance of Health Policy and Systems Research to accomplish the following global public health objectives related to systems research[7]:

- Provide a forum for the health policy and systems research community.
- Support institutional capacity for health policy and systems research.
- Stimulate knowledge and innovations to nurture learning and resilience in health systems.
- Increase the demand for and use of knowledge for strengthening health systems.

This emerging and vigorous area of research that is critically needed to better understand and strengthen health systems is described in **BOX 4.5**.

BOX 4.4 Health in All Policies

Health in All Policies is an approach to public policies across sectors that systematically consider the health implications of decisions, seek synergies, and avoid harmful health impacts in order to improve population health and health equity. It improves accountability of policymakers for health impacts at all levels of policymaking. It includes an emphasis on the consequences of public policies on health systems and the determinants of health and well-being.

Reproduced from World Health Organizations. Health in all Policies: Training Manual. Geneva: Author; 2015.

BOX 4.5 Health Policy and Systems Research (HPSR)

HPSR is an emerging field that seeks to understand and improve how societies organize themselves in achieving collective health goals and how different actors interact in the policy and implementation processes to contribute to policy outcomes. By nature, it is interdisciplinary, a blend of economics, sociology, anthropology, political science, public health, and epidemiology that together draw a comprehensive picture of how health systems respond and adapt to health policies and how health policies can shape—and be shaped by—health systems and the broader determinants of health.

WHO, AHPSR. Accessed February 16, 2018.

BOX 4.6   Chronic Disease Conditions Worldwide

Prevalence of diabetes worldwide

Year	2000	2030
Diabetics in the world	171 million	366 million

7.4 million: The number of people who died from cancer worldwide in 2004. Today, cancer causes one death in every eight, which was almost 7 million in 2015.

15 years: The deficit in average life expectancy for men in Eastern Europe compared with those living elsewhere in Europe in 2015. Nearly half of this excess mortality was due to cardiovascular diseases with an additional 20% due to injuries.

150 million: The number of people globally experiencing financial catastrophe due to the costs of chronic disease care and disability.

Data from World Health Organization. World Health Statistics 2008. http://wh.int/whosis/whostat/EN_WHS08_Full.pdf ?ua=1. 2008.

Finally, the WHO is concerned about the rise of chronic conditions and non-communicable diseases (NCDs) globally, as shown in **BOX 4.6**.

In their multicountry comparative health systems study, Johnson, Stoskopf, and Shi found that diseases and health conditions such as heart disease, stroke, cancer, chronic respiratory disease, mental illness, and diabetes have reached epidemic status in most countries, low-income and high-income alike.[8]

Cardiovascular disease is now the leading cause of death in the world and is the number one cause of death in all regions except sub-Saharan Africa, where the combination of HIV/AIDS, TB, and malaria have become syndemic. The WHO claims the worldwide threat is growing rapidly, predicting that deaths from infectious diseases will decline by approximately 3% until about 2025, whereas deaths caused by chronic diseases are projected to increase by nearly 20%. To better understand chronic disease from a systems perspective, the multicausation model, as illustrated in **FIGURE 4.5**, identifies many of the causal factors, determinants, and interconnections.

As shown in the model, chronic disease relates to lifestyle and the environment in which a person lives. The WHO asserts there are common, modifiable risk factors that underlie major chronic diseases. These are shown in **FIGURE 4.6** as behavioral and environmental risk factors. The figure also shows interconnections with other factors contributing to NCDs and chronic conditions. From a systems thinking perspective, each arrow in the illustration serves to identify opportunities for analyses and interventions, while the modifiable risk factors can serve as leverage points.

The WHO identifies chronic conditions as the healthcare challenge of the 21st century.[9] There is an escalating global burden of chronic and NCD and their economic impact on patients, families, communities, and governments. Unfortunately, current systems of care are not designed very well for chronic health problems. Thus, there are deficits in these systems that impede successfully managing chronic

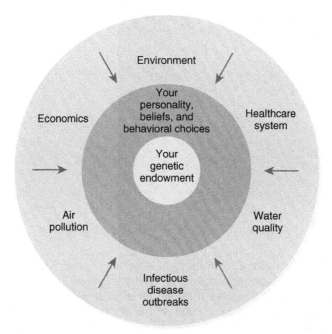

FIGURE 4.5 Multicausation Systems Model of NCDs

Source; Johnson, Stoskopf, and Shi, *Comparative Health Systems*, 2nd ed. 2018.

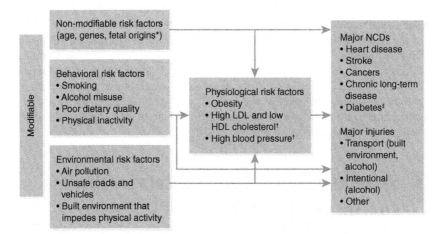

FIGURE 4.6 Modifiable Risk Factors (Leverage Points) for NCDs

conditions. Because health systems have evolved around the concept of acute care and infectious disease, with the demographic transition toward chronic conditions, these systems cannot continue to meet the needs of the population. Additionally, as long as the acute care model, based on reductionist and linear thinking, dominates healthcare systems, health expenditures will continue to escalate, while not necessarily improving population health status.[9]

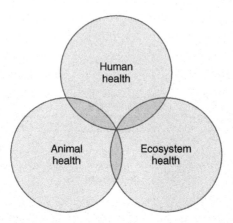

FIGURE 4.7 One Health: Human Health, Animal Health, and Ecosystem Health

Out of this concern, the Innovative Care for Chronic Conditions (ICCC) Framework was developed to help health systems improve care for chronic conditions.[9] The ICCC Framework is comprised of fundamental components within individual, organizational community, and policy levels. These components are described as "building blocks" that can be used to create or redesign health systems to more effectively manage long-term health problems and mitigate a wide range of associated disabilities and impairment to physical and social well-being. Michael Merson's book, International Public Health: Diseases, Systems, and Policies, provides a systems-based model of the ICCC Framework, as shown in **FIGURE 4.7**. The model uses the systems thinking concept of interrelatedness (labeled "links" in the model) between the community and a healthcare organization, while also showing the ever-important need for a positive policy environment. As described in this chapter (see Figure 4.2), policy development is one of the core functions of public health, and in this case, it requires the formulation of policies favorable to chronic conditions management and prevention. Systems thinking will be essential throughout as the need to map linkages, identify feedback loops, and build sustainable partnerships continuously emerge.

▶ Systems Science at the Centers for Disease Control and Prevention (CDC)

There are myriad ways in which the CDC has embraced and utilizes systems thinking. One example is the use of Behavior Over Time (BOT) Graphs. This systems thinking tool is sometimes called time series or trend graphs where epidemiologists can present longitudinal data. Many public health problems such as rates of smoking, childhood obesity, increase in opioid use, and teenage pregnancy are often communicated this way. The CDC embraces systems thinking as it encourages transcending events to determine trends, systemic structures, and mental models that produce events. Systems methods such as BOT graphs may illuminate structural elements of a complex system, including relationships between factors, feedback loops, and delays between cause and effect. Using systems science tools such as BOT graphs, systems dynamics models, and network analyses can help public health professionals understand, describe, and intervene within complex systems to address challenges. A major goal of applying systems thinking by the CDC is to develop comprehensive, practical solutions to complex challenges that influence population health outcomes, while also being mindful of intended and unintended consequences of actions, interventions, and policies.[10]

Syndemics as Systems Thinking

These include the Syndemics Prevention Network, supported by the CDC, which studies how recognition of mutually reinforcing health problems (e.g., substance abuse, violence, and HIV/AIDS) expands the conceptual, methodological, and moral dimensions of public health work and ways of thinking about health as a system. The Network advances research and activities in response to the growing impact of interacting epidemics.[1,11] The concept of syndemics is very much within the systems thinking paradigm, as originator and medical anthropologist Merrill Singer describes it as an emergent phenomenon. He asserts that rather than starting with the part (a pathogen, disease, or condition), we should begin by looking at the whole (the full array of health and social problems suffered by an individual or community). In doing so, we must assess the nature of the interconnections among the parts, including the intricate ways in which they promote and reinforce each other to create a complex web of entwined health and social challenges.[11] Political scientist Sylvia Tesh, in her work on political ideology and disease prevention policy, advocates a shift in public health from "silos to systems" and observes that "modern public health has moved far beyond simple linear and reductionist understanding of disease causation to the recognition of the need for multi-causal models."[11,12] Elaborated further by Merrill, such systems thinking models, sometimes displayed as complex interacting nodes connected by many bidirectional lines or as a series of overlapping or concentric circles, include numerous factors that contribute to a disease or health condition. One example of the concentric circle imagery is the multi-causation model, previously shown in Figure 4.5, which identifies many contributing factors.

▶ One Health Initiative

Another very promising area of public and global health that has its foundations in systems thinking is the One Health Initiative, which focuses on the connections among human, animal, and ecosystem health, as illustrated in Figure 4.7.

Richard Riegelman and Brenda Kirkwood, in their book titled *One Health: From AIDS to Zika*, contend that human health is dependent on animal health and the health of the ecosystem. "We're all in it together, it's no longer just about the human race; it is about the health of all living things."[13] The One Health Initiative, involving the CDC, WHO, and World Animal Health Organization, is defined as "the collaborative effort of multiple health science professions, together with their related disciplines and institutions—working locally, nationally, and globally—to attain optimal health for people, domestic animals, wildlife, plants, and our environment."[13] As illustrated in **FIGURE 4.8**, One Health is designed to serve as an "umbrella organization" to create a system of communication and collaboration

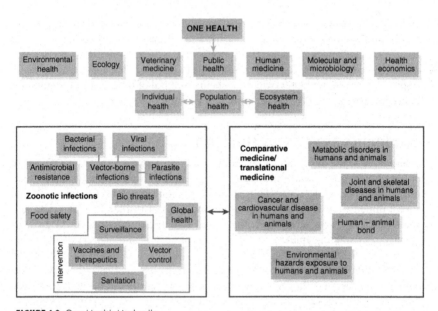

FIGURE 4.8 One Health Umbrella

Reproduced from One Health Initiative. About the One Health Initiative. http://www.onehealthinitiative.com/about.php.

and address complex systemic challenges at the interface of humans, animals, and the ecosystem.

Additionally, One Health involves a wide spectrum of health consequences ranging from infectious diseases to allergies, NCDs like cancer or asthma, and mental health. The initiative suggests a number of general areas of focus that need to be addressed. Each of these could be enhanced by embracing systems thinking and utilizing systems science methods as follows:

- Strive to minimize the extent and progression of climate change.
- Pay attention to the impacts of "industrial" production of animal products.
- Reduce the mismanagement and mistreatment of livestock.
- Use judiciously antibiotics in humans and animals.
- Increase collaboration among human, animal, and environmental health professionals.
- Anticipate pandemics and the development of effective response systems.

▶ Conclusion

Public and global health has, perhaps more than other domains, embraced a systems perspective with systems thinking being evident in the various agencies, programs, and initiatives. Furthermore, public health educators and professional associations see systems thinking as a vital core competency that can span the full range of public health activities and responsibilities. Systems thinking is empowering to public health practitioners, researchers, policymakers, and most importantly to the people and communities being served. The favorable biases toward engagement of all stakeholders—valuing the interdependence of people, organizations, and communities; understanding interconnections and multi-causality in health and disease; and having the enlightened awareness that naturally flows from systems thinking—all combine to inform and improve public health.

The next section presents interviews of two public health leaders and one global health consultant, all of whom provide their insights on systems thinking and share examples from their own experience.

▶ Systems Thinker Interviews

Interview 4.1: County Health Department Director Interview

Sanford D. Zelnick, DO, MS

Director, Sumter County (Florida) Health Department

Florida Department of Health

Tallahassee, FL

Interviewed by Dr. James A. Johnson

Do you consider yourself a "systems thinker"? Please explain.

Dr. Zelnick: With all modesty, yes, I do. Again, this probably sounds immodest, but the first principle is the ability and will to think, meaning the ability/facility to develop an idea or concept, as opposed to merely following direction. Specifically, it was my occupational medicine training at the University of Cincinnati, where I was strongly encouraged to do original research and for the first time, I truly began to think creatively in this sense.

Meaning no disrespect, much of my career prior to this was the application of defined treatments for medical conditions as a family physician. It takes some thought obviously to make the correct clinical diagnosis, but after that, the treatments are usually well defined. For example, you can look up how to treat high blood pressure, diabetes, depression, etc. When doing the original research, you are frequently trying to answer a question that has not been asked. The skill set is quite different.

I will mention that the first idea or thought was the most difficult to come up with. Now, these ideas happen frequently and I have come up with five to six major ideas, as concerns public health.

After one develops a skill to think in this way by creating an idea, the second step is to consider the possible ramifications, an important part of systems thinking, often considering the social and political context. This takes experience and judgment. There are several good ideas that may not be implemented for this reason. It takes judgment, timing, an ability to listen, and a little bit of self-created "luck" to bring a good idea to implementation in an operational sense.

How is systems thinking as a competency beneficial to the practice of public health?

Dr. Zelnick: If you do not understand the ramifications of an idea, you cannot serve as an effective advocate for health. In public health, there are many viewpoints, all of which must be respected and considered, when advocating for a specific approach to an issue and sometimes, I have been surprised by what I have heard at times but again, all views must be valued and respected. Whatever the other opinions are, I feel better that I heard them at the onset. It is a collaborative function and one that values a sense of autonomy on the part of the public, even if you may disagree. I believe it was Stephen Covey who said, "First seek to understand," referring to other viewpoints. When I develop an idea, an epiphany—as I jokingly mention it to my senior staff—I develop a wide circle of opinions and consider those opinions well before I embark on advocating a measure.

In what ways can systems thinking be integrated into program planning?

Dr. Zelnick: I believe a checklist or similar tool can be developed, although with experienced planners, much of this comes naturally.

The initial considerations are the impacts—the measurement of any potential goods versus potential harms or risks—of any specific program upon the population under consideration, including special or vulnerable populations. What evidence is there of effectiveness or of harm?

Is the thought under consideration something that would win public support? How would it be explained?

What resources are required, in terms of personnel, funds, training, monitoring of effectiveness, of a specific program, and is this expenditure worth it, as this often competes with other priorities set either by the public or higher headquarters?

How have you adopted systems thinking in your organization? Community? Describe an example you are proud of.

Dr. Zelnick: We have not developed a checklist but the basic concepts I am describing are routinely followed in a successful public health program.

Often, the ideas come to me serendipitously (almost by accident but I have come to realize, as I have stated, that it is no accident). A long time ago, I worked in Washington for the Air Force Surgeon General as chief of Occupational Medicine, and he told his staff then that if we just answered our email and responded to other inquiries that reached our desks, we really were not doing our jobs, and I took his point to what I do.

Shortly after I assumed my position here, I happened to be reading on the Internet an article in the West Orange County (Florida) newspaper about the problem of drowning deaths in children, and the rate of drowning is much higher in black children, which is what this article was speaking to. I did additional research and found that the CDC supported the thrust of much of what was written in the article.

I did more research and located a book titled Contested Waters by Jeff Wiltse, which describes the experience of minority communities in a sociopolitical context (I would highly recommend reading).

I began to think about water safety programs, particularly in Florida, because we are surrounded on three sides by water and so much defined by it, in terms of our recreation and economy.

In my small rural county, there were no such programs. I asked my staff, particularly my environmental staff as they have a role in permitting public pools, to identify any pools that could be in our county, which could be used for training. At this time, I was developing a relationship with the local superintendent of schools. As luck would have it (and I don't mean to belabor this, but I believe you make your own luck), the local school board complex was once a former mental health treatment facility and they had a pool that was rarely utilized.

After discussions with Sumter County Government and the Sumter County Schools, in 2012 we developed a program for two weeks of instruction in basic swimming/water safety, for children ages 3–12 years. Our water safety instruction team are all trained and certified by the American Red Cross. The program is extremely popular, training between 150 and 200 children every summer. In fact, one summer we trained 285 children. As the program matured, we found a second pool on the north end of the county that we were permitted to use for free, which is closer to our urban center.

I am fortunate in that Sumter County Florida is an area of rapid economic growth, we are the seventh fast growing county in the United States, and I was able to convince Sumter County Government to largely subsidize this program. We charge only $10.00 for two weeks of instruction, which is much less than what it costs to run the program but is what many families in the more rural parts of this county can afford.

As a health department (and a small one at that with only 40 people), again with all modesty, we directly train more children in water safety than any health department in Florida.

We intend to publish our experiences about this in a peer-reviewed journal someday (we are gathering data in Excel and have received permission from the Florida Department of Health Institutional Review Board). Due to the creative work of one of my staff members here, we even have the possibility/potential to develop a national data set, as concerns water safety training.

I have had several other ideas, some I have brought to fruition, some I am trying to bring about, but it would be too much to write about.

Why do you believe systems thinking has not easily been adopted more broadly in public health?

Dr. Zelnick: If you really want to accomplish something meaningful, you must understand the ramifications of your actions and garner support. So, I believe these processes are utilized among successful public health practitioners, but they are not standardized into a checklist or formal function perhaps to the extent they should be. I think it would be useful for junior health officials and could be developed into a teaching/mentoring program.

Any ideas about how we can create a systems thinking culture in public and community health?

Dr. Zelnick: I think the first step is creating a supportive atmosphere, an atmosphere that stimulates thought and discussion. Ideally, systems thinking is something that should happen at the program level in a health agency, where program managers are encouraged to develop such a capacity/skill as they grow as health officials. In Florida, we have a mentorship program, understanding every county is unique in terms of its outlook, its priorities, and its challenges. Often, I find, it is difficult for program managers to see beyond a somewhat constricted horizon. I am not sure about the reason for this. Here, in this small health agency, I have strongly encouraged my staff to think in the ways I have written about and suggest their ideas. I solicit their thoughts about ideas I have come up with. Just last week, I had an idea about testing the well water of persons who are diagnosed as positive for *Helicobacter pylori* infection.

Interview 4.2: Community Health Administrator Interview

Celia S. D. Thomas, MPA
Chief Operating Officer
Alternatives For Girls
Detroit, MI
Interviewed by Dr. James A. Johnson, March 2018

Do you consider yourself a "systems thinker"? Please explain.

Ms. Thomas: I consider myself a "systems thinker." With nearly 30 years of experience in Child Welfare, Human Services, and Organizational Leadership, I've evolved to understand the significance of researching how the world works, including how we interact with each other and what factors impact others to generate positive or negative results. Essentially, I view systems thinking as the ability to look beyond the trees and recognize the forest. I firmly believe that we can use systems thinking approaches to resolve challenges.

How is systems thinking as a competency beneficial to the practice of public health?

Ms. Thomas: Understanding the types of systems at play and how these systems work helps the practitioner to operate effectively, practically, and often preemptively within and across systems to address public health. Furthermore, embracing a social model of health in conjunction with the standard medical model of health care is a beneficial approach to preventing disease and illness and enhancing public health. For example, in my current job, we're integrating multiple individual, small-scale systems to form a macro-level, diverse system to prevent teen pregnancy.

In what ways can systems thinking be integrated into program planning?

Ms. Thomas: In one of your books, Dr. Johnson, you tell us that "in many cases, communities are often resource-rich and coordination poor." Across my state, while the rate of teen pregnancies is slowly decreasing, there are disparities in the decreases with girls of color lagging behind their white counterparts. In my organization, we believe that resolving this teen pregnancy issue and the disparities necessitates a community-level and community-wide approach, and there are interdependencies across the systems. Therefore, we are integrating multiple small-scale systems to form a macro-level system to prevent teen pregnancy. Furthermore, we anticipate that using systems thinking framework will yield positive results by decreasing the disparities and that this model of service can be scaled.

How have you adopted systems thinking in your organization? Community? Describe an example you are proud of.

Ms. Thomas: Over the last decade, I have been involved with considering and implementing systems of care in the human services arena. This work started with identifying strengths and limitations across the service providers/resources available in my community and has continued with the implementation of client-friendly, client-focused case management supports to help participants of the systems navigate the systems. In this work, Social Network Theory plays a strong part in demonstrating how studying the relationships and the methodology of interaction is crucial for viable change. In my current position, this is especially true for working with teens, who place high emphasis on their social networks, social identity, and social norms. Furthermore, this theory justifies the organization's use of networks to promote health behavior change in a way that increases the likelihood of long-lasting change. The incorporation of systems thinking into this work is also providing the community with the chance to view health care outside of the traditional biomedical focus and apply more rounded, interconnected focus to include social determinants of health and address the related issues with a view toward investing in human services and public health models of longer-lasting wellness and stability.

In 2016, my organization received validation that taking a systems approach (and effectively explaining our work) was the right approach when we secured multi-year federal funding to develop a plan for a randomized control trial of our "homegrown" leadership skills development training as a curriculum to prevent teen pregnancy. The training involves the following: use of peers to "teach" a range of topics such as adolescent development, college and career preparedness, healthy parent–child relationships, healthy peer interactions, leadership and sex education; collaboration with community partners (schools, teen-friendly health centers, community centers, and enrichment programs, etc.) in order to provide a "buffet" of services for at-risk teen girls to receive support designed to address their range of needs; case managers to support and guide the at-risk girls through a case plan; and a series of follow-ups over an 18-month time frame.

As we conduct this rigorous evaluation project, our hypothesis is that there will be a statistically significant difference in avoiding pregnancy between the girls who participate in our curriculum and the control group. We also anticipate that participation will provide the intervention group with increased knowledge and skills to access services and resources to be healthy and productive adults.

Why do you believe systems thinking has not easily been adopted more broadly in public health?

Ms. Thomas: Leading and participating in systems thinking requires collaborating partners to think outside the box and recognize that being in silos is counterproductive to positive outcomes for clients. In the world of serving youth, many of the nonprofit human service providers embrace the teens' slogan "Nothing about us, without us," which simply means that providers should embrace our target population by including them in research, collaboration, and intervention efforts. We place high value on giving the youth a voice and a seat at the table as we work to ensure that their needs are met and that they are able to break away from their at-risk status. Systems thinking requires trust among partners to be open to sharing resources and coordinating efforts in spite of any real or perceived risks of losing clients or funding. Perhaps, on some level, public health has been in a responsive mode with simply applying the medical models of care versus being in a proactive mode with embracing the whole person approach as defined by a systems thinking approach. I believe that the more we understand systems, the more we can anticipate our target populations' behavior and work within systems to improve quality of services, and ultimately, the quality of life for participants.

Any ideas about how we can create a systems thinking culture in public and community health?

Ms. Thomas: As we survey the global landscape, we can find successful examples of systems thinking as the standard operating procedure. In one of my leadership classes, I learned that leadership is the art of mobilizing others to want to struggle for shared aspirations. In order to create and drive a systems thinking culture in public and community health, leaders in these areas must understand and embrace the facets of this approach, they must be willing to share details regarding the triumphs and trials of this movement, and they should be comfortable with managing change in order to work toward change.

Interview 4-3: Global Health Consultant Interview

Cathy Robinson, DHA, IHC, MSA, MLS(ASCP)CM
Global Health Consultant
International Medical Laboratory Services
Interviewed by Dr. James A. Johnson, April 2018

I know of your global health consulting work and a recent international research project you completed. How many countries have you worked in? Give us a few examples.

Dr. Robinson: I have worked in 40+ countries. The 193 UN states are divided into five regional groups. I have worked in one or more countries in each of these five regions. Vietnam, Kenya, Tanzania, and the Ukraine are among my favorites. I still maintain contact with colleagues in these countries.

Do you consider yourself a "systems thinker"? If so, please explain.

Dr. Robinson: First, I must explain that I am currently and have been a medical laboratory scientist for many years as well as an international laboratory consultant. My responses are based on my perspective as a laboratorian and consultant. My international experience includes working with many heavily burdened countries to improve the accuracy of laboratory testing in identifying the HIV/AIDS status of the global citizenry. To contain and then stop HIV/AIDS, laboratories must improve their accuracy in reporting positive and negative HIV results, analyzing patients' specimens to begin treatment, and monitoring side effects from the antiretroviral treatments. Laboratory services are a vital subsystem within the global system to conquer HIV/AIDS and establish standardized health care for all.

I must respond yes, I do consider myself a "systems thinker." As I begin a new project in a country, I automatically look at the big picture and begin categorizing all the individual components within the whole project. Each component has its own goals and objectives and interacts with all other components in multiple ways. I also try to imagine where obstacles may arise between the components and design feedback loops to act as monitors. Each of the 'parts' influence the outcome, so carefully designed metrics help to identify obstacles before they cause delays or project failure.

For example, when I agree to develop a workshop on a specific topic, I first discuss the country's need for the information and how participants will use the information (the big picture). Next, specific goals and objectives are identified and agreed upon with the in-country experts. From this basic design, subsystems emerge: How many participants can the workshop accommodate? What are the knowledge and skill background levels of the participants? Will participants adhere to attendance requirements during the workshop? What level of participant knowledge should the materials be—basic, intermediate, or advanced? Feedback loops monitor each of these subsystems. Are the participants engaged and do they interact with each other as well as with me? If yes, the positive feedback loop tells me that the optimal level of materials is correct. If not, the negative feedback loop indicates that I should increase or decrease the depth of the materials presented. Other subsystems include selecting culturally appropriate examples for explanation of concepts, using politically correct suggestions in moving forward with improvement plans, ensuring availability of resources for implementing new procedures and new equipment, and many others. I must always be aware of cultural requirements, such as proxemics and acceptable voice quality. Nonverbal cues from the participants alert me if I make an error. Facilitating workshops in a language other than English has its own subsystem, with critical loops indicating understanding of the materials. All translators are not equally adept at translating medical terminology. Once, a presentation stalled completely due to a translation error. After a short break with the facilitators, the translators, and several participants, the error was rectified. Apparently, the Russian and the English definitions were quite different. Consensus was reached, and new terms were added to clarify the meaning. This was a workshop on best practices for specimen collection, so the definitions were critical.

As a systems thinker, I always keep in mind each country's individual requirements to reach their training goal. Each country is a subsystem in the overall system to improve global health and, as such, each system must function successfully.

How is systems thinking as a competency beneficial to your practice as a global health consultant?

Dr. Robinson: Global health is a huge and complex system. A nonlinear systems approach yields the most useful and valuable information on both the whole system as well as all the myriad of country and other subsystems. Each country I consult in has its own unique set of systems and subsystems and yet, all the systems in all the countries must work together to achieve improved global health care.

In what ways can systems thinking be integrated into program planning and evaluation?

Dr. Robinson: In designing a project with a country, all stakeholders must have input into the design, so perspectives, possibilities, and barriers are identified and discussed. Selecting appropriate metrics in the form of 'loops' for both quantitative and qualitative components ensures all the component parts are monitored to ensure each is functioning as designed.

How have you adopted systems thinking in your practice or research? Describe an example you are proud of.

Dr. Robinson: One recent project comes to mind. Country "A" was part of a multi-country Joint United Nations program, begun in 2014, working with other partners to reach the UNAIDS 90-90-90 targets. The project's aim was to diagnose 90% of all HIV-positive persons within each country, provide antiretroviral therapy for 90% of those diagnosed, and achieve viral suppression for 90% of those treated by 2020. Conducted in 2017, evaluations for measuring country progression toward reaching the first "90" goal showed that countries were not close to reaching the first "90%" target.

Country "A" had lost motivation, and their project was in disarray. I assisted with evaluating their current program design and offered recommendations to restart the program. My first step was to review each stakeholder's component part within the plan goal and ask for perceived successes and barriers. Second, all stakeholders attended a meeting where a realistic assessment was presented. Several gaps were self-identified. Each stakeholder was cognizant of his or her own mini-subsystem and where his or her gaps existed but the stakeholders were unaware of the other stakeholder's gaps. While the original design seemed well planned, there were no feedback loops identified or metrics in place to identify problems. Each system functioned within its own silo. For example, when asked to provide a list of all trainings and participants certified as nonlaboratory HIV testers, no one could find it, although they knew which partner had worked in what region of the country. To begin a new program start, the stakeholder team designed a revised work plan, assigned tasks to individuals with deadlines for completing the project and reporting to the whole team. Since the most difficult part of any project is the beginning, the team set this meeting as the begin date, thus effectively already engaging everyone.

To redesign their original plan, stakeholders created communication plans designed to acknowledge and share individual progress and barriers with the whole group. A simple yet effective feedback loop was simply to schedule frequent meetings between stakeholder groups. The metric assigned to measure the meeting component was documentation by dissemination of minutes to all stakeholders. One member agreed to be the project champion and maintain a file of all activities and meetings for easy reference. A root cause analysis was substituted for the previous personal blame approach to challenges or errors with the benefit of encouraging open discussions and sharing of ideas between stakeholders. Discussions were either face-to-face meetings or email exchanges; both facilitated the team approach to solving issues. Now, frequently scheduled emails go to all project members to keep everyone updated on the project progress. As their advisor, perhaps the most important aspect of improvement was the engagement of all team members, their confidence level, and their willingness to share challenges and find solutions together. With the feedback loops and metrics in place, individual motivation soared. The transformation from silo- to team-based efforts revitalized the program. Members are now interacting with each other and the project is moving forward to achieve the first "90" target. Inserting feedback loops allowed individual subsystems to interact with each other in ways not previously considered. Country "A" represents only one (14%) of seven countries collaborating on this initiative. However, each country must design its own subsystem to interact with the other six for all countries to function in the overall system of reaching the 90-90-90 targets.

For this country, all the necessary information was available if only the member knew where to look. Communication pathways and loops provided the missing link.

Any ideas about how we can create a systems thinking culture in global health?

Dr. Robinson: First, creating a "systems thinking culture" involves a move from linear to nonlinear thinking and planning, which is confusing to many people. To others, the fear of giving up certainty and allowing nonlinear thoughts and ideas is too great to even attempt. People must have confidence in themselves and their groups. At the same time, they must appreciate new approaches to success that may be the result of learning from previous failure. This takes time and positive reinforcement loops. For global health to function effectively, all players need to understand the proposed changes and see how those changes will enhance their roles and benefit their organization and, in turn, benefit health care worldwide. Perhaps the world has already begun to accept systems thinking in global health, but there are inefficient feedback mechanisms currently in place that need readjusting. Also, change takes time.

References

1. Shi L, Johnson JA. *Public Health Administration: Principles of Population-Based Management.* 3rd ed. Sudbury, MA: Jones & Bartlett Learning, 2014.
2. Riegelman R. *Public Health 101: Healthy People-Healthy Populations.* Sudbury, MA: Jones & Bartlett Learning; 2014.

3. Institute of Medicine. *The Future of Public Health*. Available at: https://www.nap.edu/catalog/1091/the-future-of-public-health. Accessed February 12, 2018.

4. Johnson JA. *Introduction to Public Health Management, Organizations, and Policy*. Clifton Park, NY; 2013:184.

5. Draper S. *Systems Thinking: Unlocking the Sustainable Development Goals*. Forum for the Future. Available at https://www.forumforthefuture.org/blog/systems-thinking-unlocking-sustainable-development-goals. Accessed April 10, 2018.

6. World Health Organization (WHO). *Systems Thinking for Health Systems Thinking*. Geneva: WHO Press; 2009.

7. World Health Organization (WHO). Alliance for Health Policy and Systems Research. *Bridging the Worlds of Research and Policy*. http://www.who.int/alliance-hpsr/about/en/. Accessed January 25, 2018.

8. Johnson JA, Stoskopf CH, Shi L. *Comparative Health Systems: Global Perspectives*. Sudbury, MA: Jones & Bartlett Learning; 2018.

9. World Health Organization (WHO). *Innovative Care for Chronic Conditions*. http://www.who.int/chp/knowledge/publications/icccreport/en/. Accessed January 10, 2018.

10. Center for Disease Control and Prevention (CDC). *Using BOTS in Systems Thinking*. Available at https://www.cdc.gov/Pcd/issues/2018/17_0254.htm. Accessed January 25, 2018.

11. Singer M. *Introduction to Syndemics: A Critical Approach to Public and Community Health*. San Francisco, CA: Jossey-Bass; 2009.

12. Tesh S. *Hidden Arguments: Political Ideology and Disease Prevention Policy*. New Brunswick, NJ: Rutgers University Press; 1988.

13. Riegelman R, Kirkwood B. *One Health: From Zika to Ebola*. Sudbury, MA: Jones & Bartlett Learning; 2018.

CHAPTER 5

Systems Thinking Cases

▶ Introduction

This chapter was added to enrich the readers' understanding of systems thinking by seeing it in action through cases studies and demonstrating the use of various systems tools and concepts. The cases were selected to reflect a diversity of settings, sectors, communities, and countries. This includes cases from hospitals, clinics, public health agencies, community-based organizations, and a global health consulting firm. The range of authors is equally diverse with the fields of nursing, medicine, health administration, epidemiology, public health, business, medical science, and social science all represented. The "common denominator" is that each of the case contributors embraces systems thinking in their professional practice, continuous learning, and life perspective. As mentioned previously in this primer, systems thinking is a mental model. Beyond the cognitive realm, it is a paradigm that is shifting how various professions and disciplines view the world. When we change our view, we change everything.

Some of the themes, either implied or overt, that run through the cases are the significance of "social determinants of health," the importance of collaboration, the central role of stakeholders, and the favorable bias toward looking at the whole, and not simply the parts. Furthermore, the reality of interconnection, interdependence, and intercommunication is very evident. As with all cases, written to enhance learning about a subject, readers must draw their own conclusions, inferences, and apply the "lessons" to their own work or life situation. Finally, as a practical matter, we have provided systems thinking tools such as causal loop diagrams, root cause analysis, mapping, and archetype identification to demonstrate their utility and diversity of application.

Our wish is that the chapter and its incredible, is transformative in its impact, as it infuses your understanding of systems theory with the realization of the efficacy of systems thinking in action.

James A. Johnson, PhD, MPA, MSc

$\mathcal{P}$ CASE 1: A Collaborative Systems Approach to Health Care

Written by Caren Rossow, DHA, MBA

Modified From Earnest and Brandt. (2014). *Aligning Practice Redesign and Interprofessional Education to Advance Triple Aim Outcomes* and the World Health Organization. (2010). *Framework for Action on Interprofessional Education and Collaborative Practice.* Geneva, Switzerland. Retrieved January 23, 2018, from http://www.who.int/hrh/resources/framework_action/en/.

Amelia is a young Somali refugee woman with juvenile-onset diabetes. From her apartment, she tests her blood sugar level. The reading, which is electronically transmitted to the Federal Qualified Health Clinic (FQHC) where she is a patient, activates a system of health care and learning that has been carefully created around her. She is a member of an alliance, a team of clinicians, university faculty, health professionals-in-training, and members of her community collaborating to keep her healthy.[1]

Recently, the local university and the FQHC were integrated into a major regional health system, creating an interprofessional learning and healthcare delivery partnership along with the Somali Community Development Alliance (SCDA). The SCDA works with the healthcare alliance to obtain culturally competent health care for their community, as well as role models and an education pipeline for a new generation of Somali health professionals. In turn, the university is graduating healthcare professionals who learned their skills in the community and understand the importance of collaboration, while achieving the Triple Aim—enhancing the patient experience and population health while decreasing overall costs.[1]

Interprofessional education is defined when two or more professions learn about, from, and with each other to enable effective communication and improve health outcomes.[2] In this context, a professional is all-encompassing that includes individuals with the knowledge, skills, and ability to contribute to the physical, mental, and social well-being of a community.[2]

Medical, nursing, pharmacy, and occupational therapy students from the university learn together, rotating in interprofessional teams to complete their training in an integrated healthcare system that incorporates ambulatory clinics, patient-centered medical homes, and acute care and transitional care units within a community setting. This system setting allows the health science students to build healing relationships with their patients and families, work with traditional and nontraditional providers of care (community health workers), immerse themselves into different cultures, receive an opportunity to coordinate care across various healthcare settings, and participate in systems improvements.[1]

Today, Amelia's blood sugar level is elevated. The results were transmitted electronically via cell phone to the FQHC, triggering an alert in the electronic health record as well as a notification to Amelia that someone from the FQHC would call her. At the FQHC, the nurse preceptor scans the alerts for the day, and on noticing Amelia's elevated blood sugar level, she meets with the interprofessional team. From the meeting, the pharmacy student and Somali community health worker call Amelia on her cell phone, communicating with her in her own language that they have been working with her nurse practitioner preceptor to determine the amount of medications she should take today and provide her with the required dose of insulin.

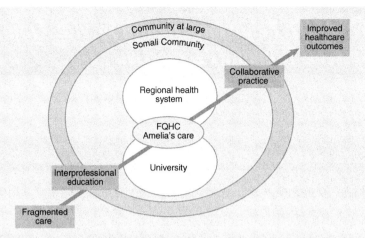

FIGURE 5.1 Community and Health System Domain

Modified from Earnest and Brandt. (2014). Aligning Practice Redesign and Interprofessional Education to Advance Triple Aim Outcomes and the World Health Organization. (2010). Framework for Action on Interprofessional Education and Collaborative Practice. Geneva, Switzerland. Retrieved January 23, 2018, from http://www.who.int/hrh/resources/framework_action/en/.

While on the phone, Amelia relays that she is experiencing other symptoms. They gather all the information and begin to develop a plan of care. After review by her family physician, Amelia is called to come into the FQHC for lab work. A few hours later, the pharmacy student and community health worker call Amelia notifying her that she has a urinary tract infection. They clarify the severity of the infection, question her regarding any allergies to medications, and verify the location of her pharmacy. Education is provided on taking an antibiotic as well as plans for follow-up care. Later that day, the interprofessional healthcare team huddles to discuss several events of the day. The pharmacy student briefly shares Amelia's history and her plan of care focusing on medications, diabetes care, Somali culture, and the role of interprofessional healthcare team members. Concentrating on systems issues, the team members discuss the FQHC's diabetes care goals and their roles in collecting and analyzing data on the care processes and outcomes. The next three days, a member of the interprofessional healthcare team call Amelia for follow-up care. Her blood sugar level has returned to a normal range, and she is feeling much better. **FIGURE 5.1** illustrates the community and health system domain interconnected with interprofessional educational and collaborative practice ultimately improving the health outcomes of the entire domain.[1]

The FQHC has surpassed its performance goals with reducing costs by approximately 20%.[1] The entire system as a whole has benefited by a decrease in hospitalizations and emergency department utilization. Most importantly, the Somali community has achieved health, wellness, and survival statistics that are indistinguishable from other wealthy suburbs nearby.

References

1. Earnest M, Brandt B. Aligning practice redesign and interprofessional education to advance the triple aim outcomes. *J Interprof Care*. 2014;28(6):497-500.
2. World Health Organization. Who.int. Framework for action on Interprofessional Education and Collaborative Practice. http://www.who.int/hrh/resources/framework_action/en/. Geneva, Switzerland. Published 2010:1-62. Accessed January 23, 2018.

🔍 CASE 2: Behavioral Health Services from a Systems Thinking Perspective

Written by Debbie Lull, RN, BSN, MSA, DHA, FACHE

Contributed by Debbie Lull RN, BSN, MSA, DHA, FACHE

Recently, the community health needs assessment of a regional healthcare system (RHCS) identified mental health as one of its primary concerns, followed by diabetes, heart disease, and obesity. Due to its pervasive penetration of concern throughout the community, the RHCS recognized the many challenges going forward. One challenge is that mental health is certainly a specialty left to expert professional providers. Therefore, contractual arrangements were necessary to obtain reputable professionals at the state level. These specialists now work within the RHCS, partnering with the local team members of the behavioral health service line. Goals for every metric were established in the top decile performance levels, aligning with the rest of the organizational goals. In fact, the full psychiatrist staffing model is the result of robust physician recruitment efforts. Additionally, renovations were underway to redesign the behavioral health unit to accommodate those who are more acutely ill and aggressive in nature. This, in turn, will create not only a safe place for the more violent patients but also for other vulnerable patients as well as the team members working in the unit. Current dialogue among leaders of the RHCS aims to establish a brand-new department to be built in 3 years. Therefore, the behavioral health service line plans are at the forefront of senior leaders, community stakeholders, and other legislative personnel, raising awareness of the dire need to address behavioral health concerns of the community. This is not unique to this community. In America, challenges continue as well as sources of optimism as it relates to addressing mental health issues.[1]

There are common characteristics for the healthcare leader who contemplates addressing behavioral health issues. Leaders should become adept at applying systems thinking competencies in an agile manner, and they need to focus not just on the parts of the system but rather the whole system when addressing issues.[2] **FIGURE 5.2** provides a conceptual model of addressing events, patterns, and behaviors over time, and systems, structure, and dynamics that would apply to resolving issues in behavioral health services.

There are too few healthcare systems addressing mental health issues, as the one described previously with aspirational systems thinking, using a whole systems approach rather than a linear, stovepipe model. Sustainable models for the provision of behavioral health care, its characteristics (either present or not), and its many stakeholders require a systems thinking approach. For example, the characteristic, self-stabilizing, is what behavioral health services should strive to become. Mental health best practices and exemplary outcomes are not as prevalent throughout networking and benchmarking opportunities as other disciplines in the medical field. Goals are needed to form a more robust resolution to the Triple Aim. Social factors, such as caregiver support and transportation, are needed for the success of the Triple Aim, better care, better health, and lower cost.[3] Therefore, if the state funding is decreased for mental health entities in the community, is the goal of achieving the Triple Aim obtainable?

One characteristic that is currently pervasive is program-following or policy. In other words, once the patient connects with a psychiatrist, an assessment is

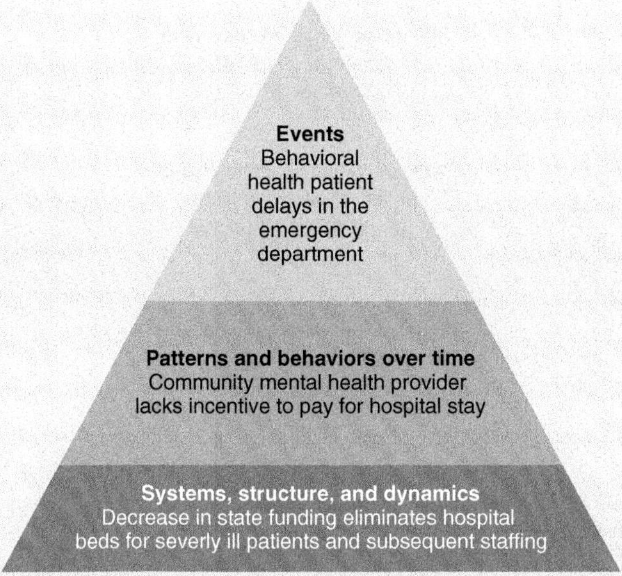

FIGURE 5.2 Conceptual Model of Behavioral Health Issues Related to Behavioral Health Patient Placement in an RHCS

Adapted from Johnson JA, Anderson DE. Systems Thinking for Health Organizations, Leadership, and Policy. Austin, TX: Sentia Publishing; 2017: 28.

completed along with a treatment plan. This positive characteristic fits appropriately in a feedback loop of communication between the patient and the psychiatrist. Another positive characteristic is environment modifying. Each level shown in Figure 5.2 has its own method of modifying its own environment to be successful. The emergency department modifies its policies to accommodate the patient awaiting disposition. The community mental health entity becomes creative with its funding to maintain budget. Finally, the state withholding funds is necessary to allocate funding with a higher priority.

Using Causal Loops

Causal loop diagrams are a well-established method to visualize the complexity of a system to better highlight actions that will lead to positive results. These diagrams provide framework for analyses, generate predictions, explore intervention effects and gaps.[4] **FIGURE 5.3** displays a causal loop diagram, utilizing the same behavioral health services issue as in Figure 5.2. A reinforcing loop is established between the Emergency Department (ED) and community mental health and between state funding and community mental health.

When the community mental health screener does not approve funding for inpatient hospitalization, the feedback loop returns to the ED, and patient placement is delayed until both parties agree to the appropriate level of care. Additionally, when the state limits funding to the community mental health entities, less funding is available to pay for hospitalization, and placement will not occur until funding is secured by

(continues)

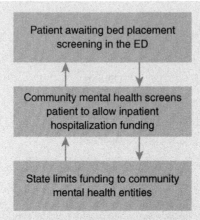

FIGURE 5.3 Causal Loop Diagram Displaying Behavioral Health Issue

the state. All three entities are relying on each other to coordinate care for this very vulnerable population.

Case Commentary

A more systems thinking approach to the behavioral health issue is to assess each characteristic. For example, many negative feedback loops and knowledge about external environments, such as the community mental health program and the state policy, are valuable resources by which to gain knowledge of the issues and to self-stabilize. Addressing population health needs as it relates to mental health will assist in achieving the Triple Aim.

   To assure effectiveness and sustainability within the health system, other variables can be addressed by including key stakeholders at the local, regional, and state levels. Acquiring reimbursement, recruiting providers, and integrating new services proves to be beneficial for organizations going forward.[5] Keeping this in mind as it relates to each characteristic of the issue, offering services that will gain revenue and enhance reimbursement from payers is a value-add. Recruitment of exemplary psychiatrists and other providers of behavioral health care will add to the care that the community expects of its local RHCS. Integrating new services, such as telepsychiatry, to supplement care for those patients in remote locations adds to the care as well.

References

1. Giled S, Frank RG. Economics and the transformation of the mental health system. *J Health Polit Policy Law.* 2016;41(4):541-558.
2. Johnson JA, Anderson DE. *Systems Thinking for Health Organizations, Leadership, and Policy.* Austin, TX: Sentia Publishing; 2017:28.
3. Shier G, Ginsburg M, Howell J, Volland P, Golden R. Strong social support services, such as transportation and help for caregivers, can lead to lower health care use and costs. *Health Affairs.* 2013;32(3):544-551.
4. Joffe M, Mindell J. Complex causal process diagram for analyzing the health impacts of policy intervention. *Am J Public Health.* 2006;96(3):473-479.
5. Clark R, Jeffrey J, Grossman M, Strouse T, Gitlin M, Skootsky S. Delivering on accountable care: lessons from a behavioral health program to improve access and outcomes. *Health Affairs.* 2016;35(8):1487-1493.

🔍 CASE 3: How Causal Loop Diagrams Could Be Used to Create Better Assessments

Written by Doug Anderson, DHA, MSB, FACHE

Introduction

Winters come and go. However, clinics are showing up on every corner as if the 1980's gas wars have been reincarnated. Patients with minor care and emergencies (real or perceived) come and go randomly through urgent care clinics (UCC). In many cases, these clinics serve as a referral base or "spoke" back to a major facility or "hub"—ORG-X. In this case, during the winter period, only 76% of patients passed through the UCC in 30 minutes or less. This metric was significantly below the organization's 95% target and notably shortfall compared to previous winters. The demand for UCC services increased by only 2% during this time. A marginal increase should not tip any system into critical mode, especially when seasonality is entirely predictable. However, the "hub's" health administrator team became concerned. So, why did the crisis happen? Why do winter crises keep happening? Moreover, why do they seem to get worse each year? [Cause and effect dialogue should have started].

Problem

Some mused, the demand for UCC services was due to climate change. The UCC is one part of the ORG-X health system. Some health administrators suggested that the UCC was a part of the greater community health system but scoffed, "not our responsibility…." [boundaries]. The demand for UCC services depends on the capacity of other departments [parts of the system] of ORG-X's hospital and other institutions within the health ecosystem: surgical centers, ancillary services, community health and social care services, phone lines, care documentation, and so on. Surmising about climate change or scoffing at boundaries discounted the fact that ORG-X's health system is part of the greater ecosystem. Without a common understanding of the whole system or ability to search for events and patterns in the environment, such as patients becoming frustrated and going elsewhere, ORG-X's health administration team concluded that the issue was seasonality [systems thinkers would have explored the dynamics of the environment].

ORG-X's health administration team did not adequately question their assumptions. The demand for UCC services was not understood. There is an assumption: More people are insured with more complex health problems and visit the UCC during holiday season when downtime is available. However, the data prove otherwise. Visits and admissions—many of which require follow-up care—are higher in the summer, while the number of patients with complex problems does not vary from season to season.

The Root Cause

Each ORG-X department and each UCC are separate, with their objectives, pressures, budgets, and targets. The UCC health administrators rarely observe the patient's journey end-to-end. Healthcare administrators do not take the time to identify potential failure points across the system [cause and effect] unless a single metric, such as wait time, becomes an outlier [isolated versus integrative decision-making]. The 30 minutes or less UCC waiting target brings its challenges. As a yardstick to gauge flow capacity, it is an effective measure. However, it is widely considered a simple "line in the sand" between success and failure and only measures the UCC's performance, not ORG X's. They fail to correlate the issues elsewhere in ORG-X, such as billing, availability (and response time) of on-call providers, beds, nursing staff ratio, or access to ancillary services satisfaction. ORG-X encourages short-term optimization of UCC resources, rather than long-term

(continues)

solutions [dysfunctional archetype] to the wider problem in the system—the patient's journey and experience of care.

In reality, the heart of the UCC winter crisis was a systems-wide supply problem compounded by a lack of internal coordination. The flow capacity of health services as a whole was not being planned. Flow capacity reduces access to most ORG-X services during winter—managers, staff, and support workers take Christmas breaks. This situation puts more pressure on resource capacity and creates a downstream spiral: quicker turns (and shortcuts) of patients, medical supply outages, and records availability due to slow turnaround or update times. The whole system gets jammed, yet the wait time metric becomes the trip wire for hip shooting rather than exploring the real cause and effects, such as more competition across the street, frustrated patients who sought treatment elsewhere, and demotivated the staff.

Short "Feel Good" Solutions: Lack of systems thinking drives actions and decisions that do not alleviate the problem. First, when planning service capacity, senior managers tend to look at only one aspect of resource capacity, not the whole system. Assuring enough rooms, staff, and support is essential. A closer look at flow capacity would identify how decisions made during the Christmas holiday's staff vacation would impact the flow and other metrics [delays that are often hidden]. Fencing off resources and reducing schedules [Archetype: Tragedy of the Commons] in other areas do not relate to demand or reflect when people fall ill, visit the UCC, or leave ORG-X's health system [delayed reinforcing loops].

As the winter crisis emerges, the UCC goes into firefighting mode—transferring patients to their departments in ORG-X shifts the burden [Archetype: Shift the Burden] elsewhere. ORG-X's health administrators reallocate resources to other parts of ORG-X unbeknownst to the UCC, thus reducing capacity in other parts of the system. The lack of coordination leaves attempts to improve the system disjointed, overloading staff with conflicting workloads. To address what one health administrator referred to as "systemness," ORG-X's health administrators created overly complicated solutions by setting up a screening and priority systems to manage urgent demand but this led to more frustration.

Sustainable Solutions

More understanding and action are required. To tackle the root causes of the winter crisis, ORG-X's health administrators need a thorough understanding of:

- How different components of health ecosystem interact with each other. If the UCC providers determined that referrals to social services were an option, they may not know of the available resources.
- The actual levels of demand coming into the system at each entry point and how work flows through the ORG-X system as a whole. Assessing delays in patient flow and external and internal influences would have been more beneficial.
- Constantly assess the differences between flow and resource capacity.
- Lack of staff, poorly coordinated holiday schedules, and staff dissatisfaction leading to employment elsewhere may have been the real causes.
- Understanding how the system caused variations in demand and capacity.

Case Commentary

This case illustrates why health administrators must embed systems thinking skills across their workforces, so they can maximize organizational performance with systems thinking. Experienced systems thinkers apply some concepts and tools to understand thoroughly how whole systems work. An example of a "whole-system" problem—one where lack of systems thinking means failure to identify the root causes and think in circles, rather than straight lines. The concepts and tools visually communicate how potential solutions affect the whole organization or community. Although there are many different tools for systems to work, *causal loop diagrams, archetypes, computer simulation software, and micro-worlds or scenario analysis* are typical. In this case, *causal loop diagrams* should have been used to show the interrelationship of a system over time, behaviors of variables, and poor decision-making. These variables relate to capacity, supply and demand, bottlenecks, and constraints represented by delays and feedback loops. This case illustrates how systems thinking impacts organizational decision-making during predictable time periods.

Many operations in the healthcare ecosystem can be viewed as complex adaptive systems. Many organizations are not equipped to identify the root causes of performance issues and encourage sustainable improvements. Typical top-down management and "siloed" approaches fail to understand the whole system. Using "whole-system" metrics to assess ORG-X's delays across time would have presented a more holistic viewpoint. Assessing metrics over time, rather than department-specific or static updates, provides a holistic picture of the situation. ORG-X's team should have measured process behavior in real time, and looking for delays in the system would have resulted in better decisions throughout the system.

Systems thinkers *think* in terms of circular reinforcing and balancing feedback processes or casual loop diagramming. As shown in **FIGURE 5.4**, ORG-X's health administrators should have addressed the causes and effects of these delays at various parts of the organizations and at the health administration levels. The reinforcing loop is based on growth or movement in a process, while balancing loops tends to limit growth or movement and generate resistance in reinforcing loops, causing changes in direction. ORG-X's winter UCC crises is a case in point, beginning with ORG-X's health administrators' own thinking by not addressing a "whole-system" problem, thus failing to embrace the underlying causes. ORG-X's health administrators should have created medium- and long-term strategies to guarantee the capacity to meet demand in every part of the system, at the right time, without unnecessary delay; coordination is required.

Properly executed, systems thinking provides a view of the whole organization. Org-X's processes to assess demand and supply in the context of external dynamics did not exist. Doing so created a false archetype. Furthermore, archetypes or stories

ORG-X style of solving problems

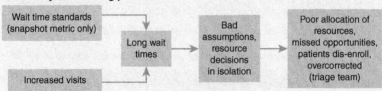

Feedback: Illustrating how causal loop diagram produce a fix that failed

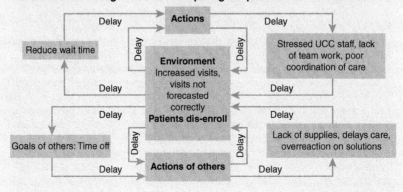

FIGURE 5.4 How ORG-X's Lack of Systems Thinking Led To Poor Decisions

(continues)

about cause-and-effect loops help explain reality in a systems way. ORG-X's health administrators should have taken the time to understand their interdependent processes from their patients' and frontline employees' standpoints. The archetypes illustrate how inattention and siloed thinking can disrupt organizations. Many of ORG-X's archetypes represented "vicious" balancing and reinforcing loops. Involving staff who represent the entire "patient's journey" aims at designing a better system because eventually, the staff must implement the system. Specific mental models or archetypes seem to occur repeatedly.[1,2] The system archetypes thus become tools for learning and also analyzing the various social structures that seem to exist in organizational and personal lives.[1,2] Encouraging systems thinking as part of continuous quality improvement and strategic planning should be an extension of the ORG X's culture.

References

1. Senge PF. *The Fifth Discipline: The Art & Practice of The Learning Organization*. Revised ed. New York, NY: Doubleday; 2006.
2. Meadows DH. *Thinking in Systems: A Primer*. White River Junction, VT: Chelsea Green Publishing Company; 2008.

$\mathcal{P}$ CASE 4: How Systems Thinking Can Identify Delays in Dysfunctional Processes

Written by Doug Anderson, DHA, MBA, LFACHE

Introduction

Virginia Mason uses the Virginia Mason Production System, which is inspired by the Toyota Production System (TPS). Although Virginia Mason has used production system methods in all departments, the case of its spine center is instructive for its results and the challenges it faced. A study of 137 patients reported that these patients were referred to Virginia Mason over a 10-month period, of whom 100 had been recommended for lumbar spine fusion by a surgeon outside Virginia Mason. After reviewing the patients' medical charts and other information, a panel of Virginia Mason experts determined that a nonoperative treatment—instead of surgery—was more appropriate for 58% of the patients [informational and perceptual delays].

Problem

The spine center was encouraged to restructure its processes due to concerns about long wait times and high costs. The center began by value stream mapping the clinical pathways for its patients and discovered that care was inconsistent—some patients received advanced imaging, for example, magnetic resonance imaging (MRI) tests and specialist care, while other patients directly received physical therapy [physical and informational delays]. Also, the current payment system can be an impediment. In the spine center, for instance, the institution began to lose money after it adopted the new clinical approach. The institution was paid for high-cost imaging studies that were conducted less frequently, and the institution was not paid for reasonable follow-up care, such as telephone consultations, which it was conducting more often [transactional delays].

Solution: Isolated surgical case management decision-making can result in inappropriate treatment that is a disservice to patients, a waste of healthcare sources, and an unnecessary cost for the patient and the provider [dysfunctional archetype].[1] To improve, the clinic reviewed the literature on back pain treatments and developed standard evidence-based processes. Under this process, patients with noncomplicated back pain were directed immediately to physical therapy, and MRI scans and intensive evaluation were reserved for more complex cases. This new process aligned with clinical evidence, showing that imaging for lower back pain is often overused, especially in clinical situations where it is unlikely to improve outcomes [reduced informational and perceptual delays].[2] Multidisciplinary collaboration empowered experts from multiple specialties to recommend the use of surgical and nonoperative treatment options.[1] To sustain the improvement initiative, it had to negotiate with local insurers and employers to establish a new payment system [reduced transactional delays].[3]

Sustainable Solutions: The solution to high-reliability challenges is to understand and address the underlying broken processes and take a systems approach in doing so.[4] Moreover, given the complexity of clinical care, initiatives to add to the clinician's current workload are unlikely to succeed. Instead, significant and sustainable improvement requires reconfiguring the environment, systems, and processes in which healthcare professionals practice.[5]

Outcomes: Virginia Mason found this way of delivering care reduced wait times, improved outcomes, and reduced costs.[3] Benefits include more value-added time with providers, greater safety, less delay, and timely treatments minimize variation in care. These benefits also include less rework and reduction of waste in administrative processes. In turn, more opportunities to move to the next level of the value proposition emerge, and savings can be reinvested to support the organization's mission or community.

Case Commentary

Health administrators must be able to respond to the broader context or system of health care and quickly pinpoint dysfunctions, such as delays throughout the process of care and how to provide optimal health care. Systems thinkers must assess the "end-to-end" system, including parts of the system outside a department and organization. In this case, Virginia Mason Health System transformed management practices by adopting exemplars from other industries, ultimately increasing the quality of care by implicitly applying systems thinking. Their team and systems thinking helped proactively identify three types of *delays* in dysfunctional processes throughout the episode of care. *Transactional delays* are procedural or habit-forming guidelines that often slow down a process. *Informational delays* result in communicating information about physical changes, causes and effects, policy, and procedures. *Perceptual delays* result when individuals misinterpret or discount messages and fail to take appropriate action.

To help, exemplary practices such as the TPS adopted from manufacturing sectors can result in better patient health outcomes. In this case, Virginia Mason Health System transformed management practices by adopting exemplars from other industries, ultimately increasing the quality of care by implicitly applying the systems thinking in the form of delays. Other studies found that management practices were associated with improved care process measures and lowered mortality for heart attack patients.[3] Systems thinking helped proactively identify delays in the dysfunction processes.

A systems approach can reduce the burden of work that clinicians face while providing improved safety, quality, and value. Virginia Mason's experience reveals the challenges in adopting systems approaches. The number of *delays* throughout the system was complex yet revealing once the entire system was mapped out. Implementing evidence-based systems as a strategy to reduce delays across the organization requires a cultural shift and supports transformations.

This experience also highlights the multiple factors limiting the use of broadly spreading systems approaches. To adopt systems approaches more widely, health administrators should develop a systems thinking mind-set to explore all forms of delays. Examples such as coordinating care within and outside the health system would result in increased capacity and would balance considerations of cost awareness and

(continues)

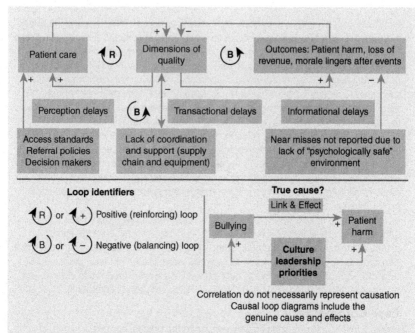

FIGURE 5.5 How Causal Loop Diagrams Focus on Root Causes

risks in population-based care before, during, and after episodes of care. To achieve the objectives to identify potential system errors, delays, and bottlenecks, systems thinking tools must be applied, as shown in **FIGURE 5.5**.

References

1. Sethi R. Virginia Mason study shows team method prevents overuse of spinal fusion surgery. 2017; https://www.virginiamason.org/virginia-mason-study-shows-team-method-prevents-overuse-of-spinal-fusion-surgery.
2. Group GSW. The "Top 5" lists in primary care: meeting the responsibility of professionalism. *Arch Intern Med.* 2011;171(15):1385-1390.
3. Blackmore CC, Mecklenburg RS, Kaplan GS. At Virginia Mason, collaboration among providers, employers, and health plans to transform care cut costs and improved quality. *Health Affairs (Millwood).* 2011;30(9):1680-1687.
4. Hoffman A, Emanuel EJ. Reengineering us health care. *JAMA.* 2013;309(7):661-662.
5. IOM. *Best Care at Lower Cost: The Path to Continuously Learning Health Care in America.* Washington, DC: National Academy of Sciences, Institute of Medicine (IOM); 2012.

How Barriers or *Downstream Spirals* Prevent Adoption of Systems Thinking

Intuitively, most health administrators understand the idea behind *downstream and upstream spirals*. Many health administrators find themselves in a *downstream spiral–cycle* of self-defeating thinking such a being held hostage to health system's dynamics. The *downstream spiral* is a metaphor for decline (a drowning "stock"), a self-reinforcing balancing loop process depleting something of value and moving downward. A *downstream spiral* can be described as a cycle of deterioration, as players withdraw resources from the system or stay in a comfort zone or silo thus reducing performance prompting more withdrawals later.[49] Health administrators cut maintenance budgets due to financial pressure, which results in more breakdowns and lower quality, rising costs and lost members, only to lead to higher financial pressure—a *downstream spiral.*[49] **FIGURE 5.6** provides an illustration of the upward and downward spiral metaphors.

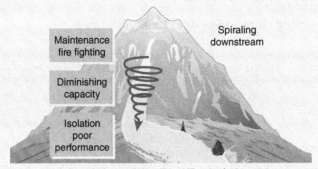

Maintenance fire fighting

Spiraling downstream

Diminishing capacity

Isolation poor performance

Restrictive policies (Dam)/fixed mind set

Aspirations (see forest and trees)/agile mindset

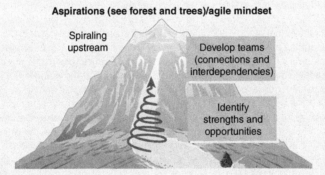

Spiraling upstream

Develop teams (connections and interdependencies)

Identify strengths and opportunities

FIGURE 5.6 Illustration of Upstream and Downstream Spirals Metaphor

From the case studies and interviews, systems thinking is being applied. However, based on the literature barriers exist. So do solutions. Barriers to widespread adoption present increased the risk of more dysfunction in organizations or barriers to health system transformation, or *upstream spirals.*[49] Systems thinkers know teams and organizations can multiply their impact by reducing delays, friction, waste, and unintended consequences.

References
49. Spiral Metaphor. Created by author Douglas E. Anderson, 2018.

🔍 CASE 5: Systems Thinking for Nonprofit Initiative to Prevent Adolescent Pregnancy

Written by Celia Thomas

Introduction
This case study focuses on a Michigan nonprofit, Alternatives For Girls (AFG) and its community-level initiative on adolescent pregnancy prevention through the

(continues)

application of learning via a "home-grown" leadership skills training course.[1] The study identifies and describes the common systems characteristics involved in adolescent pregnancy prevention efforts. This report also describes how systems thinking is being used to assure effectiveness and sustainability.

Connecting Human Services to Health Care

In the human services field where a lot of the work with clients often appears unrelated to health outcomes and funding is often difficult to secure because of this, AFG has worked tirelessly to help healthcare leaders—who are focused on the Triple Aim of (1) refining patient care experiences, (2) improving population health, and (3) decreasing per capita healthcare costs and funders who are focused on maximizing the use of the funding dollars to understand how its human services programming addresses a myriad of needs within the community. AFG has always advocated for the inclusion of Social Determinants of Health (SDH) in addressing population health care. SDH includes influences such as the physical environment within which people live, their socioeconomic status (SES), education, availability of support networks, and access to health care.[2] This advocacy really encompasses systems thinking, "a transformational way of understanding and approaching community-based solutions."[3]

Two very simple examples of how AFG has demonstrated systems thinking is through the formation of a girls running team among preadolescent girls in our after-school tutoring program to help the girls find fun ways to exercise and decrease their chances of becoming and/or remaining obese and introduce yoga to the girls and young adult women in the runaway/homeless shelter so that the young ladies learn how to handle stress and stress-related physical and psychological illnesses.

Over the last year, AFG's efforts at linking the Triple Aim with SDH are taking hold and yielding success as evidenced by the increasing partnerships we are developing with local health providers and insurers such as Blue Cross, Blue Shield, Trinity Health, and Molina. In fact, a Mobile Dentist visits the AFG building to provide access to general, nonemergency dental care for girls and women from nearby communities. In October 2016, AFG was one of 14 organizations across the United States to win a competitive, multi-year bid from the Department of Health and Human Services, Administration for Children and Families, Personal Responsibility, and Education and Innovation Strategies to assess the effectiveness of the agency-developed leadership skills training course on preventing teen pregnancy.[1]

According to the Kaiser Family Foundation,[4] there has been a decrease of all high school students who reported having had sex and decreases in teen pregnancy, births, and abortions over the last 5 years. However, recent data show that rates of unintended pregnancy and sexually transmitted infections (STIs) among adolescents and young adults in the United States remain higher than those in other developed nations and are much higher in some racial and ethnic minorities and in different areas of the country, as follows:

- Of 47% reporting ever having had sex, 48% were males and 46% were females.
- Black teens (60%) were more likely to have had sex than white (44%) and Hispanics (49%).
- Approximately 14% of black students and 6% of Hispanic students began having sex before the age of 13 compared to 3% of white students.
- Approximately 13% of female teens and 17% of male teens had more than four sexual partners in their lives.
- Approximately 34% of high school students were currently sexually active (have had sex with at least one person in the previous 3 months).

Data from the Michigan Department of Health and Human Services indicate that in 2015, the pregnancy rate for females between the ages of 15 and 19 years in the state was 31.6 per 1000.[5] However, when assessed by race, across the state, the rate was

23.2% for whites and a whopping 66.3% for blacks. Furthermore, in Detroit where there are 23,717 female teens (19,960 blacks, 3,016 whites), the overall pregnancy rate in 2015 was 77.7% with the rate for blacks being 82.5% and that for whites being 1.3%.

Study Design

Over the next 4 years, with the development of the AFG Evaluation Plan in 2017, the organization is targeting at least 600 girls between the ages of 14 and 19 years living in Detroit to conduct a rigorous, randomized, controlled trial aimed at assessing the effectiveness of its leadership skills training course on preventing teen pregnancy. A primary factor in this venture is that the intervention is multifaceted, systems thinking, not just based on providing medical care (doctor's visits, birth control, and testing). The leadership training course will be 30 hours long with topics that range from understanding and developing leadership skills for teens; adolescent development, health and healthy relationships; understanding the responsibilities and risks of having sex; to education and career readiness. The girls will be contacted to obtain outcome information at 6 months and 12 months after the start of intervention. The primary outcomes being assessed are absence of pregnancy and use of birth control.

AFG bases its work on the theory of planned behavior; if the teen girl believes unprotected sex is risky and will interfere with her goals in life, she is more likely to think of unprotected sex as a bad idea and will seek to avoid unprotected sex. The organization has identified and built in a number of feedback loops (balancing, reinforcing, and interrelated) and effects and developed a diagram that mirrors the Johnson and Anderson "How the Health System Should Work" model during the planning phase of the intervention.[3]

Systems Thinking

Resolving this community-level teen pregnancy issue/disparity necessitates a community-wide methodology, and there are interdependencies across the systems. Furthermore, recognizing that a systems thinking approach increases the likelihood of resolving the issues and providing sustainable results, AFG is utilizing a systems approach with this work. The organization is integrating multiple microsystems to form a macrosystem in a variety of ways, as follows:

- Working with area high schools and community centers to run groups at their locations
- Developing memoranda of understanding with health clinics and primary care doctors to meet general health needs, pregnancy testing, testing for sexually transmitted infection (STI) and human immunodeficiency virus (HIV) testing of the participants during intervention and up to 12 months post-intervention
- Funding case managers to support participants through this intervention. Johnson and Anderson tell us that "in many cases, communities are often resource-rich and coordination poor"[3]; therefore, AFG believes that youth, in particular, will need case management supports to navigate the systems
- Launching a public relations and community education series by engaging all forms of media to raise awareness at the highest levels (with municipalities, funders, and politicians, etc.) as well as on the very basic levels (with potential participants, families, neighbors, etc.) regarding this public health issue

Case Commentary

In this work, Social Network Theory plays a strong part in demonstrating how studying the relationships and the methodology of interaction is crucial for viable change. This is especially true when working with teens who place considerable emphasis

(continues)

on their social networks, social identity, and norms. Furthermore, this theory justifies the organization's use of networks to promote health behavior change in a way that increases the likelihood of long-lasting change. The application of systems thinking in this work is also providing the community with the chance to view health care outside of the traditional biomedical focus and apply more rounded, interconnected focus to include SDH and address the related issues with a view toward investing in human services and public health models of longer-lasting wellness and stability.

To date, AFG has had success in engaging partners with the effort. However, they are mindful that committing on paper is different from action. Moreover, even within the span of the first year of planning, one organization that promised to provide HIV and STI testing has indicated that they have lost their funding for the STI testing and can only test for HIV, so AFG has had to engage more partners in this area. Therefore, the plan is for the project's director and others to continuously reach out to partners using quarterly meetings to keep them apprised of the progress with respect to connecting the teens to their resources and overall support.

As AFG embarks on this journey of encouraging openness and connecting systems and subsystems for the purpose of preventing teen pregnancy, the organization is hopeful that the journey will be able to secure/maintain funding and move toward scalable programming along with effective, systems-changing, and sustainable results to enhance our community's ability to keep the teens in our community engaged and healthier.

References

1. Alternatives for Girls Evaluation Plan: 2017. https://www.acf.hhs.gov/fysb/resource/2016-preis -grant-awards. Accessed August 3, 2017.
2. Heiman HJ, Artiga S. *Beyond Health Care: The Role of Social Determinants in Promoting Health and Health Equity*. The Henry J. Kaiser Family Foundation: 2015. http://www.kff.org/disparities -policy/issue-brief/beyond-health-care-the-role-of-social-determinants-in-promoting-health -and-health-equity/. Accessed August 3, 2017.
3. Johnson JA, Anderson DE. *Systems Thinking for Health Organizations, Leadership, and Policy*. Austin, TX: Sentia Publishing; 2017.
4. Sexual Health of Adolescents and Young Adults in the United States. The Henry J. Kaiser Family Foundation. http://www.kff.org/womens-health-policy/fact-sheet/sexual-health-of -adolescents-and-young-adults-in-the-united-states/. Accessed August 3, 2017.
5. Michigan Department of Health and Human Services. Pregnancies by Outcome and Fertility, Abortion and Pregnancy Rates by County for an Estimated Population of Female Michigan Residents, Age 15–19. https://www.mdch.state.mi.us/pha/osr/abortion/pregbycoteen.asp. Accessed August 12, 2017.

🔎 CASE 6: Using Systems Thinking to Provide Fundamental Solutions to a Community Challenge

Written by Ogunneye Yetunde, MD

In Nigeria, primary health centers (PHCs) are present in each of the local county areas, and the local government authorities are directly responsible for them. However, the State Ministry of Health finances and supervises the standard operating procedures and guidelines for the delivery of services at the primary care centers. In the major cities, in addition to the public-funded PHCs, there are several private facilities that can provide primary care for people within its community. In the rural locations, there are fewer healthcare professionals. Urban areas are preferred because of the social and cultural attractiveness and access to basic amenities. As a result, there is a significant imbalance of healthcare facilities and health professionals in the rural and urban communities.

The majority of the people in the rural location have little or no education, and they live below the poverty level with minimal wages because they are mostly small-scale farmers and fishermen or they practice one form of animal husbandry. They can be classified as a population of low SES and consequently, a poor social determinant of health. In spite of all their inadequacies, health resources are in limited supply from the government to cover the overwhelming needs of this indigent population. A leader with systems thinking skills is inevitable in this context—inadequate healthcare workforce and healthcare facilities—to implement sustainable healthcare programs.

Every year, the state government posts new physicians to the county's PHC as their first primary assignment after 1 year of clinical internship. So, in 2007, I was deployed to Ifewara county PHC to work with the facility head nurse. That county is one of the poorest counties in the state with a population of approximately 2000 residents. The residents of Ifewara have some of the lowest SES indicators and some of the worst health. The PHC was the only available facility to serve the entire county. Two months into my job, I noted diarrhea caused a significant proportion of under-five morbidity and mortality. Because of the late presentation of patients to the hospital, most patients presented in the third stage of dehydration with an acute renal shutdown. Acute renal failure is harder to treat. Thus, patients spend more time in the hospital at that stage; they utilize more health resources and prevent other patients with acute conditions—malaria and pneumonia—from being admitted due to the lack of hospital beds. The PHC was at over-capacity and was unable to handle more patients. This ultimately contributed to the under-five mortality rate in Ifewara's local government.

Previously, the government has intervened by providing a mobile clinic to support the services of the PHC. These services are only restricted to outpatient care. Thus, there is still no adequate provision for gravely sick patients that required urgent stabilization before they are moved to secondary or tertiary healthcare facilities. The underlining problem in this primary health center was the overutilization of its limited resources regarding a preventable disease and the lack of a solution to control the incidence of the preventable disease that is overwhelmingly consuming the limited healthcare resources.

Providing a mobile clinic can be considered an inadequate quick fix because it did not include the care of patients requiring hospital admission, and a fundamental solution was not implemented. It also reflects "Shifting the Burden" archetype. The archetype posits that a problem symptom can be fixed by using a symptomatic solution or applying a fundamental solution. However, if a symptomatic solution is used, it alleviates the problem symptom and reduces the pressure to implement a more fundamental solution. Also, a symptomatic solution produces unintended consequences that limit the capacity to build a basic solution.[1] In this case, the mobile clinic was a symptomatic and short-term solution. The fundamental solution requires some environmental changes to improve the standard of living of the people living in Ifewara. The diagram in **FIGURE 5.7** illustrates this case narrative. The next section uses the systems thinking approach to explore the interrelationship between the factors that contribute to the high incidence of diarrheal disease in the communities in Ifewara.

Ifewara, being a rural county, has suboptimal access to essential amenities. The county suffers from shortages of water. The main sources of water for the community are rivers, streams, and wells. The community depends on farming and animal husbandry as a major subsistence economic activity. Both humans and animals primarily used the same sources of water. All these situations are possible risk factors for the occurrence of childhood diarrheal disease and other water- and sanitation-related communicable diseases.

(continues)

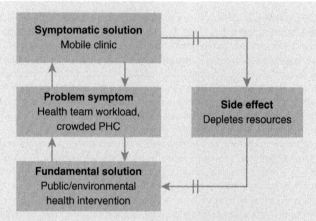

FIGURE 5.7 Using "Shifting the Burden" Archetype to Illustrate the Diarrhea Disease Problem in Ifewara

The environmental history obtained from patients at the PHC found poor living environment—space, hygiene, and sanitation facilities—to be a major problem in the community. The common factors identified included the following: a high number of persons per household; a dirt dining room floor instead of a concrete floor for the majority of families; use of river water rather than tap water for cooking and drinking; absence of a sewer for waste bath water; food left out at room temperature; and rodent infestation in the house.

The interactions of socioeconomic factors could also predispose a child to diarrheal disease. For instance, the educational status of parents influences the awareness and behavior relating to disease prevention. The quality of life, access to healthcare facilities, and environmental sanitation can all be linked to socioeconomic factors. The Causal Loop Diagram shown in **FIGURE 5.8** is used to facilitate a deeper understanding and interpretation of the interactions and feedback loops contributing to the high incidence of diarrheal disease in the communities in Ifewara.

Considering the interrelationship among the causal factors, a systems thinking mind-set is imperative for a sustainable solution, and this will require leaders to look into the community. The lack of collaboration with community systems will only prevent the building of a healthier community because the environment in which an individual lives has the greatest impact on his or her health outcomes. The overwhelming pressure on healthcare resources and patients' backlogs at the PHC is as a result of poor public health. For example, if children continuously drink from the unclean water source, medical intervention may not prevent the recurrence or reduce the incidence of diarrheal disease in the community. Thus, providing mobile clinics or building more PHCs should be considered a quick fix, which may only reduce under-five mortality, but not the incidence of the disease. The increasing incidence of the problem will eventually overwhelm the available healthcare resources and crowd out basic amenities like education—a major determinant of health. Finally, a vicious cycle is established, and a permanently impoverished community will be formed.

Case Commentary

Leaders need to know that a community such as Ifewara with no secondary or tertiary health centers in the immediate surrounding should channel its healthcare funding to initiatives designed to improve public/preventive care. This guarantees a healthier

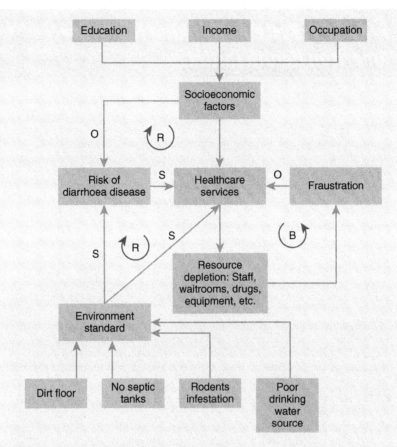

FIGURE 5.8 Interactions and Feedback Loops Contributing to the High Incidence of Diarrheal Disease in the Communities in Ifewara

community and, thus, a lesser pressure on the PHC, which aims to manage minor ailments and minimal emergencies. Therefore, the long-term plan should be focused on the social determinant of health to improve health, wellness, and community prosperity. According to medical social scientist James Johnson, the environment, as part of the multicausation model of disease, has the greatest impact on health outcomes across many populations.[2] Health leaders need to design systems affecting community conditions as part of the episodes of care as this creates a healthier community and reduces public expenses on medical care. Furthermore, it makes money available for the development of projects necessary to improve the socioeconomic indicators or other determinants of health.

References

1. Johnson JA, Anderson DE. *Systems Thinking for Health Organizations, Leadership, and Policy: Think Globally, Act Locally.* Austin, TX: Sentia Publishing; 2017.
2. Johnson J, Stoskopf C, Shi L. *Comparative Health Systems: A Global Perspective.* 2nd ed. Sudbury, MA: Jones & Bartlett Learning; 2018.

🔍 CASE 7: Systems Thinking for Native American Health Initiative

Written by Nitumigaabow Ryan Champagne

In my experience, I have the unique opportunity to lead problem-solving teams. As consultants, our customers often contract with our firm, Grand River Community Development, to help solve a problem or overcome a barrier. While their lists usually are tangible and concrete "problems," we look at the organizational systems and culture before attempting to problem solve. Often, this includes an organizational assessment. Such assessment allows our teams and the customer to see the "bigger picture" and focus on systemic or organizational issues versus program- and department-specific matters. While we employ American Indian consultants nationwide, we do not utilize consultants who are not versed in systemic solutions. These systems are often complex adaptive systems that need a problem solver who understands how relationships, systems, and practices impact organizational culture and productivity. The barrier we often face is getting the customers to understand or embrace the larger need. While I believe they understand and agree, many choose not to explore those types of solutions for fear of staff resistance, personal resistance, and/or lack of capacity to make such changes.

When thinking about systems thinking, one case example comes to mind; it was a rural northern Wisconsin tribe that had a population of about 4000 citizens. They declared a state of emergency due to the high rates of drug usage, dealing, and deaths associated with illegal drugs. The leadership was at a loss on how to combat this crisis. The crisis at hand included the following:

- Twelve deaths related to the sale, consumption, or trafficking of illegal drugs in less than 4 months
- The reported fear of leaving their house after dark due to the illegal drug trafficking and crime associated with such by elders and community members
- The report by HeadStart that 40% of the children were showing signs of developmental delay due to being born chemically addicted or exposed
- The seemingly ineffectiveness of addressing the crisis by current government programming

The first stage was to identify what the crisis entailed. This process included an analysis of the systems. The common themes that emerged included suicide, drugs, unmet behavioral health needs, and crime. The crisis factors allowed for the tribal council to come together to have a unified leadership and shared vision that the status quo was no longer acceptable. The tribal council decided to contract with our firm to gain an outside perspective and lens on the crisis state. The idea was that their staff and citizens were too close to the situation and could not maintain a systemic view required to assist in developing real solutions to combat the crisis.

Grand River conducted a Community Readiness Assessment to understand the community's current readiness and learn which community achieved a score of 2, which placed them in the domain of denial/resistance. This is normal as most individuals, whether in a social/environmental crisis state or organizational crisis state, have become desensitized to the crisis because the crisis is the status quo or "norm." Post-intervention the tool was used again to measure progress and the community achieved a score of 6.75, which raised them to a level between the initiation and stabilization domains (**FIGURE 5.9**).

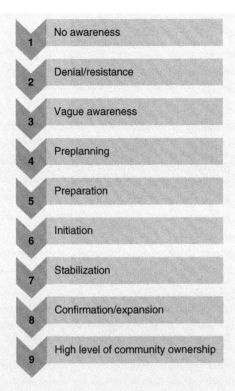

FIGURE 5.9 Stages of Community Readiness

Reproduced from Plested BA, Jumper-Thurman P, and Edwards RW. (2016). Community readiness manual. The National Center for Community Readiness. Colorado State University, Fort Collins, Colorado.

The next step in the process was to have leadership accountability. This step entailed 100% Tribal Council support of a drug-free community by submitting selected individuals to a urinalysis and hair screen, enforced "Zero Tolerance Policy" of drug usage or trafficking in government housing, and enforcement of a drug-free workplace. At first glance, this may not seem like a huge accomplishment but in a socialistic form of government where business, government, and citizenship are interconnected, this was a feat. The next step entailed a comprehensive organizational assessment, which included a systemic review of all their systems in health and human services. The review extended to collaborative agencies that impacted such systems that included the following: law enforcement; judicial, housing, education, and workforce development; and economic development. The systems assessment established baseline data, identified needs and barriers, and recommended strategies that required improvement. The assessment served as a detailed roadmap to follow to allow for systemic change.

Preparing for change requires people to change the way they view problems and solutions from a systems thinking perspective. Grand River conducted a Leadership Policy Academy that provided intensive policy training for tribal council. It allowed the leadership to start thinking of their roles as policymakers and systems change, and it led to dialogue of strategic planning and visioning. The legislators found value in this new way of thinking that they wanted something for their executive management; the Leadership Academy for Tribal Managers was created to meet this need. The tribal

(continues)

managers learned tools for addressing systemic change by engaging the community, implementing change initiatives, leading in a state of crisis, and bridging silos and strategic planning. This was the framework in which they prepared for systemic change and the human factor.

Grand River, along with the traditional tribal community leaders, started the next stage of community engagement. This stage consisted of conducting a series of listening sessions; focus groups with elders, cultural advisors, key stakeholders, and consumers; and a community input survey. This stage allowed us to learn about community perceptions and barriers and problem-solve practical solutions. This stage set the framework of visioning for the community, and their vision is what drove systemic change and community development. Understanding the interconnectedness of these systems and how the community members comprise the most vital part in solutions was critical in this process, as they are the experts of their community.

Policy development and advocacy stage allowed for: creation of policy and legislation; advocacy with federal, state, and local governments; and development of partnerships with local coalitions, state departments, and federal agencies. This stage called on system partners on the local, regional, and macro-levels to share in the solution process. This process allowed a truly encompassing systemic approach to addressing a crisis in a relatively small community. This set the context for the building alliances stage in which Grand River facilitated the process for a formal tribal state partnership and federal partnership. The tribal state partnership addressed social and health disparities, provided funding and technical assistance, and prioritized needs and development of action plan. Under the tribal law and order act, the tribal federal partnership authorized funding, training, and technical assistance development of tribal action plan—priority funding for federal agencies.

All of the previous steps were needed to be in place to allow for the final steps of strategic planning, reorganization, and implementation. The strategic planning sessions led key stakeholders and the community to recognize the need for reorganizing the Health and Human Services. The first step entailed merging 14 independent siloed programs into three main programs, the creation of Human Services Department, and the recruitment of a national expert to lead the department. The next phase was to create a Health and Human Services Division, which entailed merging the three departments into one division and centralizing the core functions and the administration, which increased efficiencies, bridged silos, and reduced costs. Post-reorganization, a formal strategic plan was adopted that allowed for the initiatives to occur, as shown in **TABLE 5.1**.

As the chart demonstrates, these were the major change initiatives that occurred due to a systems thinking perspective, which entailed the following ten-step Tribal Transformation Process: (1) Identifying the Crisis; (2) Unified Leadership; (3) Community Readiness; (4) Accountability of Leadership; (5) Organizational Assessment; (6) Policy Institute; (7) Community Engagement; (8) Policy Development and Advocacy; (9) Building Alliances; and (10) Strategic Planning, Reorganization, and Implementation. Within 3 years, the Grand River Community Development was able to assist the tribe with 21 major self-sustaining initiatives totaling over $15 million brought into the community to start up such initiatives. The annual profit/cost savings from the initiatives totaled more than $5 million.

TABLE 5.1 The System Spectrum and Key Stakeholders

Public Safety	Judicial (Zaagibaa Healing to Wellness Court)	Health Care (Clinic/Public Health)	Health Care (Community-Based Elder Disability)	Health Care (Residential)	Human Services (Crisis/Residential)	Human Services (Funding/Case Management)	Workforce Development	Corrections	Cultural
Surveillance Monitoring System	Adult (Alternative to Corrections)	Prescription Drug Monitoring System	Tribal Operated Waivers	Residential Treatment Center	Emergency Shelter	Title IV-E Pass-through Agreement – Child Welfare	Youth Build	Higher Education in the County Jail	Traditional Healing and Doctoring
Operation Pandora (Interagency Drug Enforcement Approach)	Youth (Early Intervention)	Public Health Awareness Community Campaign	Residential Care Apartment Complex	Permanent Supportive Housing	Peer Supportive Living Homes	Targeted Case Management	Small Business Development in Auxiliary Health and Human Services Vendors	Clinical Services in the County Jail	Ceremonial Roundhouse
Exclusion and Removal (Banishment)		Patient-Centered Medical Home Model				Tribal Wraparound			Family Circles – Grassroots Cultural Intervention
						Comprehensive Community-Based Services			

As the chart demonstrates, these were the major change initiatives that occurred due to a systems thinking perspective, which entailed the following ten-step Tribal Transformation Process: (1) Identifying the Crisis; (2) Unified Leadership; (3) Community Readiness; (4) Accountability of Leadership; (5) Organizational Assessment; (6) Policy Institute; (7) Community Engagement; (8) Policy Development and Advocacy; (9) Building Alliances; and (10) Strategic Planning, Reorganization, and Implementation. Within 3 years, the Grand River Community Development was able to assist the tribe with 21 major self-sustaining initiatives totaling over $15 million brought into the community to start up such initiatives. The annual profit/cost savings from the initiatives totaled more than $5 million.

🔍 CASE 8: Using Systems Thinking to Better Understand Immunization Services

Written by Eric Levielle, MPH

This case study examined the use of systems thinking to understand the growing complexity governing immunization services in Kerala, India.[1] The study explored this complex issue using an adaptive system lens. Historically, Kerala had an unusually high immunization rate of 84% in the late 1990s, although it was a state with a low economic status; however, there has been a sudden decline in immunization rates, which is a major public health concern.

After randomly selecting two districts, one with high immunization rates and the other with low immunizations rates, the data were collected from the literature, documentation reviews, in-depth interviews, focus group discussions, and observations of immunization services. To understand the data, qualitative analysis was performed and the results were placed into causal loops. **FIGURE 5.10** shows the causal loop diagram representing the factors that influence high vaccine acceptance and coverage.

Additionally, **FIGURE 5.11** shows the causal loop diagram representing the factors influencing low vaccine acceptance.

In the causal loop diagrams, factors influence vaccine rates in Kerala by facilitating the identification and understanding of unintended consequences and unexpected phenomena.

Case Commentary

Using complex adaptive systems lens through the creation of causal loop diagrams is beneficial because it shows how systems thinking concepts and methods can be applied to a complex question such as changing household acceptability to immunization and most, if not all, public health strategies.[2] It completes this by allowing public health professionals to go beyond epidemiological and economic analysis, engaging the community in the solution and accounting for cultural variation.

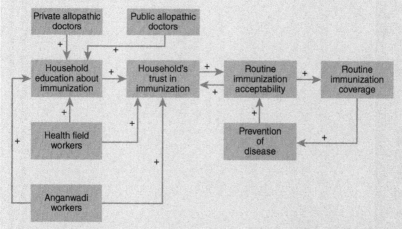

FIGURE 5.10 Causal Loop Diagram Representing the Phase of High Vaccine Acceptance and Coverage

Reproduced from Varghese J, Kutty VR, Paina L, Adam T. Advancing the application of systems thinking in health: understanding the growing complexity governing immunization services in Kerala, India. *Health Res Policy Syst.* 2014: 12(47).

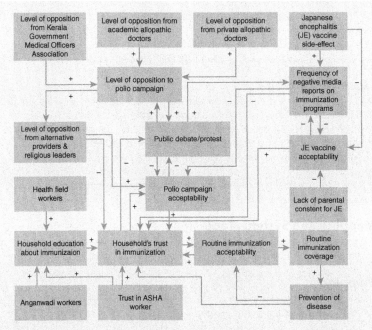

FIGURE 5.11 Causal Loop Diagram Representing the Phase of Low Vaccine Acceptance in Kerala

Reproduced from Varghese J, Kutty VR, Paina L, Adam T. Advancing the application of systems thinking in health: understanding the growing complexity governing immunization services in Kerala, India. *Health Res Policy Syst.* 2014: 12(47).

References

1. Varghese J, Kutty VR, Ligia P, Taghreed A. Advancing the application of systems thinking in health: understanding the growing complexity governing immunization services in Kerala, India. *Health Res Policy Syst.* 2014;12:47.
2. Johnson JA, Stoskopf CH, Shi L. *Comparative Health Systems: A Global Perspective.* 2nd ed. Sudbury, MA: Jones & Bartlett Learning; 2018.

🔍 *CASE 9: Health Systems Thinking Intervention for Neglected Tropical Disease*[1]

Written by Gabrielle Walcott-Bedeau, MD, MMSci, PGCME

Background

The microscopic threadlike worm (*Wuchereria bancrofti*) invaginates the lymphatic nodes and vessels where it reproduces, creating millions of microfilariae. Microfilariae are transmitted from person to person via mosquito bites. The worms become adults in approximately 6 months, and the adult worms live for approximately 6 years. When the adult worms die, the person's bodily response causes inflammation of the vessels, resulting in lymphedema (swelling) of limbs, legs, breasts, or the genitalia. According to

(continues)

the Centers for Disease Control and Prevention (CDC), lymphatic filariasis (LF) is "one of the world's neglected tropical diseases (NTDs), affecting more than 1 billion people."[2] Although most infected people are asymptomatic, 30% of infected people develop debilitating manifestations, which affect their ability to be productive.

Current Situation

The current statistics indicate that LF affects over 120.0 million people in 73 countries worldwide. However, this is a neglected tropical disease that can be eliminated. The World Health Organization (WHO) launched the Global Lymphatic Filariasis Elimination Program with a target elimination deadline of 2020.[3] In the Americas, 11.3 million people are at risk for acquiring the disease. Mass public health efforts reduced the transmission in Costa Rica, Suriname, and the Republic of Trinidad and Tobago. However, there is still active transmission in four countries in the Americas: Brazil, the Dominican Republic, Haiti, and Guyana.

Mapping as a Systems Tool

The public health strategy to interrupt transmission requires the health agency to map the endemic areas, administer drugs to break the transmission cycle, and reduce microfilaremia.

Mapping

Statistics generated by the Ministry of Health indicates the prevalence of the LF antigen in 7 of 10 geographic regions in Guyana.

Administering the Drugs

In 2003, the Ministry of Health collaborated with the Pan American Health Organization/World Health Organization (PAHO/WHO) to implement phase one of the Transmission Interruption Plan.[3] This phase included social mobilization, distribution, promotion and use of diethylcarbamazine-fortified (DEC-fortified) salt, and the monitoring and evaluating of the progress at sentinel sites. The scientific efficacy of DEC-fortified salt to reduce microfilaremia is well established and documented in pilot studies in Brazil, Haiti, India, and the United Republic of Tanzania. In fact, the DEC-fortified salt causes few or no adverse reactions when compared with the DEC tablet. As such, officials in Guyana launched a national program that introduced DEC-salt into the competitive market. This was accompanied by social marketing activities to increase consumer demand. These included television ads, health education seminars, appearances at health expositions, and door-to-door counseling.

Social Determinants of Health

Guyana is classified as the second poorest country in South America and the Caribbean with per capita gross domestic product of US $800.[1] All of the healthcare initiatives are coordinated by the Minister of Public Health and his/her ministry. Several challenges with this program were as follows:

1. The lead agency for health promotion is the Division of Health Sciences Education, which is involved in training health staff and NGOs. However, the Ministry of Health lacked sufficient health staff to coordinate mass countrywide drug/salt marketing education activities. As such, a partnership with PAHO/WHO resulted in a project launch funded by PAHO/WHO for training and development of a team specifically geared toward countrywide health education, DEC-fortified salt promotion, and active marketing and sales of the salt.

2. DEC-fortified salt needed to be imported and sold not as a drug but as a food product. As such, the Ministry of Health (MoH) partnered with the salt producers and importers to facilitate the ease of importation regulations.
3. The sales of salt decreased with disruptions to the salt supply and reduced consumer confidence after the salt became discolored (turned blue over time). The MoH increased quality control and collaborated with PAHO/WHO on a second social mobilization campaign to restock the retail suppliers and quell the concerns of the population.
4. DEC-fortified salt competed with cheaper alternatives, which were not fortified with DEC or iodine. The MoH and government partnered with importers and salt producers to increase the supply and consumer demand for the salt, as this targeted both the iodization and LF programs.

The production of DEC-fortified salt for mass treatment stopped in 2007 after the importation of approximately 900 tons of salt from the time the program launched in July 2003. In 2008, The MoH embarked on phase two, which included evaluation of phase one, identification of *hotspots* using surveillance information, Mass Drug Administration with tablets (DEC-fortified salt and albendazole), and monitoring and evaluation of sentinel sites. Once again, the Ministry of Health partnered with PAHO/WHO and the Inter-American Development Bank (IDB) for support. The MoH has even indicated that this LF elimination program is integrated with the Georgetown Sanitation Improvement Program, which was supported by both the IDB and Guyana Water Incorporated. The healthcare system in Guyana is able to achieve successful results because of its public/private partnerships. These partnerships, linked by systems thinking, not only offset the financial and human resource constraints of the country's healthcare system but also strengthen the health system's ability to reduce the burden of diseases, especially neglected tropical diseases that can be eliminated.

Case Commentary

Since this is a global disease that has long been neglected, there has been new attention brought to the challenge by the Carter Center in Atlanta, GA, where they have a Lymphatic Filariasis Elimination Program.[4] The Center assists countries, specifically Ethiopia, Nigeria, and the island of Hispanolia, to distribute medications for free to stop mosquitoes from transmitting the parasite from infected to uninfected people. Additionally, thinking of the broader system, that is, environment and lifestyle, the Center has assisted in the distribution of long-lasting insecticidal bed nets to protect pregnant women and children who cannot receive drug treatment.[4] The bed nets have the added benefit of protecting against other mosquito-borne diseases, such as malaria that affect health and well-being, as well as economic capacity.

References

1. Johnson JA, Stoskopf CH, Shi L. *Comparative Health Systems: A Global Perspective.* 2nd ed. Sudbury, MA: Jones & Bartlett Learning; 2018.
2. Center for Disease Control and Prevention. *Lymphatic Filariasis Epidemiology.* Atlanta, GA; 2018. https://www.cdc.gov/parasites/lymphaticfilariasis/epi.html. Accessed May 4, 2018.
3. World Health Organization, *Global Progress Toward Elimination.* Geneva, Switzerland: WHO; 2018. http://www.who.int/lymphatic_filariasis/global_progress/en/. Accessed May 4, 2018.
4. Carter Center, *Lymphatic Filariasis Elimination Program.* Atlanta, GA; 2018. https://www.cartercenter.org/health/lf/index.html?gclid=EAIaIQobChMIhsT39ffs2gIV0zaBCh1UMAbEE AAYASAAEgLH7_D_BwE. Accessed May 4, 2018.

(continues)

⌕ CASE 10: Developing a Systems Thinking Framework for Health Systems Strengthening

Written by Stephen Powell, MSc, Asaad Mohamedtaha, PhD, and Daniel Wyman, MD, MPH

Background

Health systems problems in the 21st century and their related impact on a nation's population at any level are rarely straightforward or unambiguous. Thus, today's health systems challenges require a new strategic and systems thinking mind-set. Systems thinking is both a worldview and a process; it can be used for both the development and understanding of a system and as the approach used to solve a problem. The competency of health systems thinking marks a dramatic shift from the linear or reductionist way of thinking used by traditional process improvement, including waste elimination methods. Unfortunately, health systems in many countries still use regressive and dated approaches that are not achieving improved health outcomes. The alternative to this is systems thinking, which challenges and empowers health leaders and their staff to assess the interdependencies among the elements or components within a system, and to seek out opportunities to generate sustainable solutions.

Leaders within health organizations operate mostly in a hierarchal structure—what might be thought of as swim lanes at best and more often silos at worst. System improvement investments are expected to yield measurable results or return-on-investment, yet when the system initiative falls short or fails, it is typically impossible to know why. Even when the initiative succeeds, it is equally difficult to scale or sustain the gains over time. Performance improvement has traditionally become a cyclical event, such as Plan-Do-Check-Act, instead of a generative journey toward continuous improvement in balance with a constantly changing delivery environment. With systems thinking, leaders and policymakers look at the whole system rather than its individual parts. They become expansive and nonlinear in thinking, rather than reductionist and linear. By looking at the whole, they are more capable of seeing interrelationships and patterns over time. They begin to understand that problems may be clues or symptomatic of deeper issues within a system or system of systems. Systems thinking challenges health professionals, leaders, and practitioners to look for root causes, bottlenecks, and constraints in ways that allow sustainable solutions to emerge. By so doing, leaders move away from assigning blame and focus on desired outcomes. In other words, systems thinking involves much more than a reaction to present events. It demands a deeper understanding of the linkages, relationships, interactions, and behaviors among the elements that characterize an entire system, and beyond. While leaders intuitively embrace systems thinking in their boardrooms and strategic planning off-site retreats, most have difficulty cascading systems thinking throughout the health delivery and operating systems. To help leaders operationalize systems thinking, we developed a Health Systems Strengthening (HSS) framework that serves as both a problem-solving methodology and a solutions-focused continuous improvement system. Although HSS may be more well developed in health systems in lower- and middle-income countries through the work of the WHO and the U.S. Agency for International Development, unique modifications are needed in more developed health systems.

Synensys Systems Strengthening Framework or S³F

S³F is built on an evidence-based framework composed of the following five integrated phases: (1) systems thinking and review; (2) planning and strategic alignment; (3) engineered change portfolio; (4) appraised, innovative solutions, fit-to-purpose, and context; and (5) sustainment (**FIGURE 5.12**).

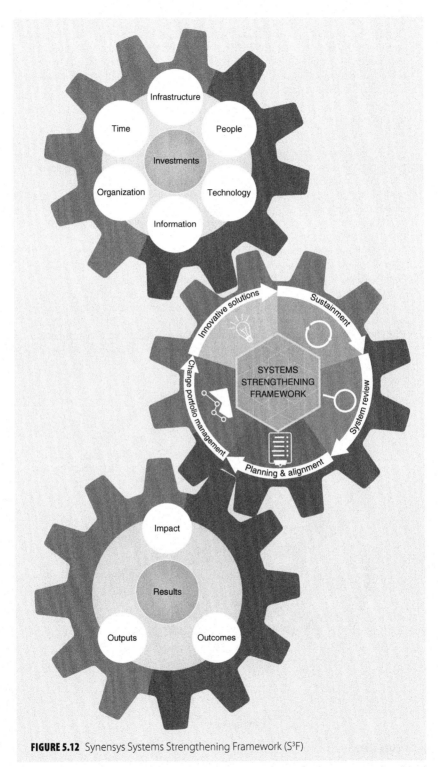

FIGURE 5.12 Synensys Systems Strengthening Framework (S³F)

(continues)

S³F incorporates more than 25 years of scientific research that has been conducted on systems thinking and design. S³F enables transformational change, using evidence-based best practices from diverse bodies of knowledge and experiences, such as the military, government, manufacturing, health, energy, aviation, and other high-risk industries. Clients who most benefit from S³F have:

- Solid mandates and drivers for transformational change and measurable outcomes
- Clear strategies and objectives to achieve their desired goals
- Accountability to deliver value for money with sustainable results

S³F components can be parsed within existing programs, as well as built into new programming, to improve efficiency, effectiveness, and economy. S³F is guided by a proven 10-point execution map that is complementary for existing execution frameworks, uses proven systems thinking tools and methods, and leverages evidence-based change management strategies (**FIGURE 5.13**).

Beginning in 2011, the U.S. Center for Medicare and Medicaid Services (CMS) launched the Partnership for Patients (PfP) quality improvement initiative in over 3000 hospitals to reduce preventable patient harm by 40% and decrease hospital readmissions by 20%. Our team, working with national organizations such as the Joint Commission Resources and State Hospital Associations in North Carolina, Virginia, Texas, New York, Florida, and New Jersey, used S³F as our foundational improvement framework to achieve the aggressive systems improvement across 10 unique healthcare-associated infections (HAIs) and conditions (HACs) such as central catheter infections, adverse drug events, and patient falls. Many past attempts to implement evidence-based care practices to reduce HAIs and HACs had achieved variable results

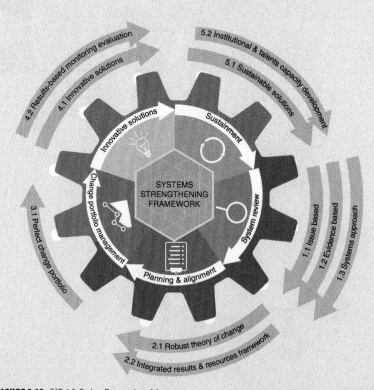

FIGURE 5.13 S³F 10-Point Execution Map

and were difficult to sustain. PfP attempted to improve systems-wide performance in numerous processes, practices, and protocols simultaneously as well as developing a stronger culture of safety by developing more engaged healthcare leaders in patient safety and quality improvement (**FIGURE 5.14**).

The initial investment by CMS in the PfP programming was $500 million over the first 5 years to produce the inputs needed based on a systems review (inputs) that included baseline infection rates, serious harm frequency, and severity of patient claims, especially in obstetrical-related harm. The programming mandate originated from the changing payment incentives from value-based purchasing (reimbursements based on higher-quality health outcomes). Hospitals were recruited voluntarily through established quality improvement relationships mostly along state or regional geographical boundaries into performance improvement collaborative cohorts using shared improvement resources (education and consultation) and centralized

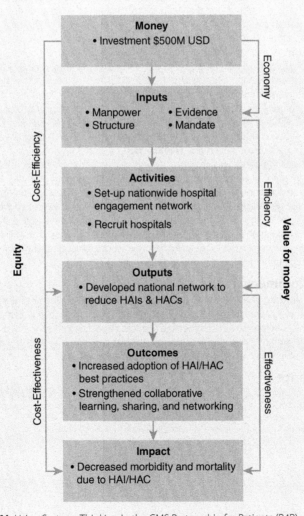

FIGURE 5.14 Using Systems Thinking in the CMS Partnership for Patients (P4P)

(continues)

data collection. Outcomes improved as hospital administrators, physicians, allied health professionals, nursing, and the public (patients, families, and advocacy groups) implemented the evidence-based practices in structured, yet fit-to-purpose ways to maximize buy in and create measurable improvement (quick wins). Ultimately, the PfP programming has saved over 125,000 lives by reducing HAIs by 3.1 million fewer infections, and $28 billion in cost avoidance due to poor quality.[1] The programming reached an estimated 33 million annual discharges. Over the 5-year period and 150 million discharges, the original investment cost less than $4 per patient discharge to produce nearly $200 per discharge savings.

Systems Thinking for the Perfect Change Portfolio

Systems thinking embraces the complex adaptive systems that are constantly changing. Most health organizations greatly underestimate the resistance to change when applying systems thinking across an organization and/or system of organizations. The implementation health information technology (HIT) systems across diverse settings is another example of using systems thinking to achieve usability, interoperability, and meaningful HIT. Most HIT implementations are one-size-fits-all, even though health systems are diverse and they perform using radically different processes within unique organizational cultures or microsystems. Again, we have leveraged change methods from developing health systems, especially from global health settings, to developing customized change theories (S³F Phase III) for each client based on a clear understanding of the stated inputs, outputs, risks, outcomes, and goals. For a global health client, we developed the change portfolio to develop a National Health Research Policy to successfully implement a comprehensive health research program with Qatar Ministry of Public Health oversight (**FIGURE 5.15**).

The change portfolio is designed to predict, manage, and promote implementation success. Assumptions are clear. Expected inputs, outputs, assumptions, outcomes, and ultimately impact are clearly articulated and updated as programming changes during the five phases and 10-points of execution within the S³F process. Mapping the expected changes creates a visible and tangible change system for leaders and other stakeholders to reference throughout the initiative, during monitoring and evaluation stages, and during post-implementation improvements for continuous learning.

Case Commentary

Using an evidence-based systems thinking framework to strengthen health systems and improve system performance can produce significant impact and healthier community outcomes with considerable financial impact. Systems thinking increases the likelihood that investments in better population health can be efficient, effective, and equitable—no matter the context or global health setting.

Reference

1. AHRQ National Scorecard on Rates of Hospital-Acquired Conditions. Agency for Healthcare Research and Quality, Rockville, MD. http://www.ahrq.gov/professionals/quality-patient-safety/pfp/index.html. Content last reviewed January 2018.

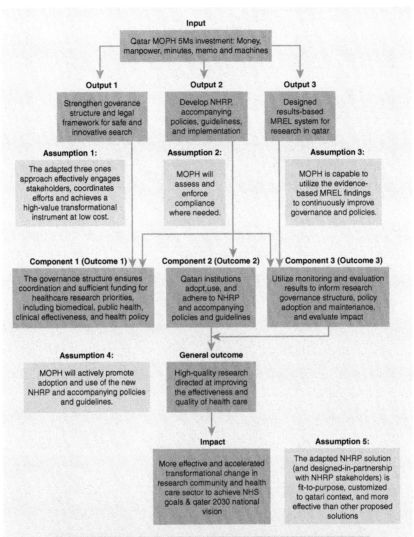

Input

Qatar MOPH 5Ms investment: Money, manpower, minutes, memo and machines

Output 1

Strengthen goverance structure and legal framework for safe and innovative search

Output 2

Develop NHRP, accompanying policies, guideliness, and implementation

Output 3

Designed results-based MREL system for research in qatar

Assumption 1:

The adapted three ones approach effectively engages stakeholders, coordinates efforts and achieves a high-value transformational instrument at low cost.

Assumption 2:

MOPH will assess and enforce compliance where needed.

Assumption 3:

MOPH is capable to utilize the evidence-based MREL findings to continuously improve governance and policies.

Component 1 (Outcome 1)

The governance structure ensures coordination and sufficient funding for healthcare research priorities, including biomedical, public health, clinical effectiveness, and health policy

Component 2 (Outcome 2)

Qatari institutions adopt,use, and adhere to NHRP and accompanying policies and guidelines

Component 3 (Outcome 3)

Utilize monitoring and evaluation results to inform research governance structure, policy adoption and maintenance, and evaluate impact

Assumption 4:

MOPH will actively promote adoption and use of the new NHRP and accompanying policies and guidelines.

General outcome

High-quality research directed at improving the effectiveness and quality of health care

Impact

More effective and accelerated transformational change in research community and health care sector to achieve NHS goals & qater 2030 national vision

Assumption 5:

The adapted NHRP solution (and designed-in-partnership with NHRP stakeholders) is fit-to-purpose, customized to qatari context, and more effective than other proposed solutions

Risks*:
1. The MOPH lacks the required resources to mainstream the new policies and guidelines.
2. Not getting full endorsement and commitment from stakeholders.
3. Project interdependency issues.
4. Delays in implementation.
5. Lack of alignment with other research policies in qatar.

FIGURE 5.15 Perfect Change Portfolio for National Health Research Policy Using Systems Thinking

Index

Page numbers followed by *b*, *f*, or *t* indicate material in boxes, figures, or tables, respectively